BLACK GIRL, KNOW YOUR WORTH!

BLACK GIRL, KNOW YOUR WORTH!

Decolonization:
The Way to Cultural Heritage
Identity Development

Dr. D'Andrea N. Robinson

CITI OF
BOOKS

CITIOFBOOKS, INC.
3736 Eubank NE Suite A1
Albuquerque, NM 87111-3579
www.citiofbooks.com
Hotline: 1 (877) 389-2759
Fax: 1 (505) 930-7244

Ordering Information:

Quantity sales. Special discounts are available on quantity purchases by corporations, associations, and others. For details, contact the publisher at the address above.

Printed in the United States of America.

ISBN-13:   Softcover   979-8-90124-014-4
                     eBook   979-8-90124-015-1

Library of Congress Control Number:

DEDICATION

This book is dedicated to ALL the beautiful Black girls who will grow into beautiful, brilliant, and bold Black women.

Acknowledgment

To God be the glory!

Thank you God for getting me through my doctoral dissertation journey which has allowed me to now author and publish this book. It has been a long road and I would not have been able to reach the journey's end had it not been for the light guiding me through the darkness.

One of the many sources of that guiding light are my ancestors who labored ahead of my time. This book is dedicated to my maternal grandmother, Edna Reddit Freeman, who recognized a need in her community and organized the first "colored" Girl Scout Troops in the Raleigh, Tennessee area in addition to founding the first early education school Kindergarten program for "colored children" in Shelby County, Tennessee. It is also dedicated to my bonus maternal grandmother, Cora Freeman, and my paternal grandmother, Alice Brown Robinson. I am also grateful to dedicate this book to Alura Freeman Wade, my maternal great-aunt, who founded ABC Preschool in Moss Beach, California and was my first teacher. In conclusion, I dedicate this book to my maternal grandfather, Minor Frazier Freeman, who was a high school teacher in Memphis, Tennessee and later moved to California to assist my parents in raising my younger sister and me; and my paternal grandfather, Alfred Robinson, Sr.

A few additional additional light sources in this journey have been my immediate family: Shout out to my parents, Minyon Freeman Robinson and Alfred Robinson, Jr., and my sister, Valerie Robinson

Allen! Additionally, my circle of "sisters" (who I've adopted over time) and my community have also been sources of light on this journey. Thank you for your understanding, love, and encouragement over these years towards dissertation and degree completion. Last but certainly not the least, Gregory K. Tanaka, you are the light that God sent from above to ensure my work entered into canon of research at this appointed time. Bless you!

This book is one of my many divine assignments and it is finished.

TABLE OF CONTENTS

Introduction

Being Ignored and Out of Place

"You are Black, and you're female! That means you have two strikes against you, and you have to work even harder at becoming the best in life!" -Alfred Robinson, Jr.

The aforementioned quote came from my dad and would cycle through my mind on repeat regularly growing up. "If you want to be the best, you have to become educated because no one can take that from you." Statements like this had a profound effect on my outlook on life, who I have become, and where I am headed. Growing up in a two-parent household with parents of the 1960s civil rights movement shaped the way I was raised and defined the value of education in my life. Both of them knew and always shared with me that education was the key to success .

As an elementary school girl, I felt out of place in my private school classroom. Academic experiences should not feel awkward because of skin color, but many times they are due to societal tensions with race. I was 1 of 3 Black students in a classroom of approximately 20 students from first to eighth grade. I have vivid memories of feeling like an outsider in a sea of White students' faces in the classroom and the entire school. My teachers were older White women who really did not exhibit knowledge or understanding of life outside of their own experiences. Nonetheless, my teachers were kind and friendly. They were cordial to me in our encounters, but when I asked my fourth and eighth-grade teachers to include instructional content that reflected me (e.g., Black culture), they simply declined my request, and that is when the relationships got uncomfortable.

Distinct memories come to mind during the month of February in these fourth and eighth- grade classrooms where my teachers enthusiastically celebrated Presidents' Month. In both grades, I requested that we celebrate Black History Month and was denied. In spite of the rejection, I persisted in pushing my teachers to include Black history and culture in our lessons. Essentially, my voice went unheard, and I was told that we would be recognizing White male role models and not acknowledging or learning Black history. This was a life-defining moment because I had come to love school for its place of self-discovery. I was seeking to discover myself while desiring to share my culture with my peers. The leadership of both classrooms stifled my voice and dismissed my moment of cultural validation.

Meanwhile, my parents were teaching me at-home lessons of being a Black girl in America, so I had some knowledge and understanding of Black history. My parents had come to understand through their own academic experiences that I was not going to learn about what being Black in America meant in school. They had the foresight to ensure my sister and I had a foundational understanding of Black men and women who were creators, innovators, and history changers. Even though my cultural validation was happening at home, my pride wanted to shine at school in my classroom with my peers.

Growing up, I used to line up my dolls in a row on the couch and played school with my younger sister. School has always been a part of my life. The concept of learning and participating in projects and activities that expanded my knowledge excited me. It never occurred to me throughout my high school and my early college years to take classes to become a teacher. However, in the midst of my undergraduate experience at the University of California, Berkeley, I decided to take a couple of education courses. During my undergraduate years, I also started to recognize that I was extremely fortunate to have been raised by parents who instilled cultural knowledge and understanding into me early.

As an undergraduate student, I started volunteering and mentoring in after-school programs in San Francisco and Berkeley. My time in the schools gave me a snapshot of beautiful children of color who were smart, capable, and excited about life. I enjoyed working in schools with young people and recognized the opportunity a position in a school had on influencing children outside of the household. My decision to become a teacher came when I recognized I could either work in the non-profit industry in relation to education or become a teacher and learn what public education was all about. Immediately after graduation, I moved to Los Angeles and took a position at a Catholic elementary school in South Los Angeles as a first- grade teacher's aide. A couple of years later, I earned my teaching credential and worked as an elementary school teacher in the San Francisco Bay Area.

I used the position of a classroom teacher as an opportunity to counter the traditional public education curricular narrative. As an elementary school teacher, I explained to my students that Christopher Columbus did not discover America and went on to explain that people already lived in North America. I encouraged my students to pursue knowledge and gain understanding outside of their curriculum textbooks. I would also tell my students year after year to critique the information they learned in school and to question the messages being shared when they did not hear both sides of the same story. As a Black woman, it became clear that public education students needed to be exposed to information that was not a part of the school district's adopted curriculum.

Instructional content is a critical factor in student learning because the content identifies and defines certain knowledge and skills that inform students of what is considered valuable. Classroom lessons reflect topics that tell students which groups of people are important and valued. Black students face challenges matriculating through school and attaining academic progress because the instructional content is often not relevant to their own lives, leading to disengagement from learning (Pringle, Brkich, Adams, West-Olatunii, & Archer-Banks, 2012). There are also teachers who lack awareness of the value of advocating for their Black students and of including the achievements and life experiences of Black students in their curricular content (Pringle et al., 2012). This division between public education and the Black student community has the potential to create a negative lasting learning identity on this particular group of students .

So why is it important specifically to address the academic needs of Black girls? Many Black little girls will eventually grow into Black women. These Black little girls are mandated to matriculate through the academic experience, whether through private or public education. In order for future Black women to be positioned as productive citizens in society and future change agents, they must be included in public education instructional focus. Therefore, I have devoted my life to preventing Black girls from experiencing the same isolation from instructional content that I felt as a student in elementary school and beyond.

I am a radical teacher, now administrator and researcher. I am a revolutionary leader because I oppose the current public education system. More specifically, I oppose the instructional content and focus of preschool through 12th-grade learning. My doctoral student journey has provided me with a greater understanding of the American education system and the intent to remove Blackness and Black excellence from public education instructional content. The founders of this nation did not want enslaved Africans to have knowledge—period.

Nonetheless, my educational journey was blessed to include parents—shout out to Alfred Robinson, Jr. and Minyon Freeman Robinson—who had the foresight and wisdom to navigate my learning experiences with Black history and culture. It is my appreciation for my parents' decision making that has helped me to recognize my own place in academia. I am the change I want to see in the American education system. I am a revolutionary researcher using my dissertation to shine a light on the need to shift public education instructional content because there are Black girls who need an academic experience that includes knowledge and understanding of self, also known as Black history and culture.

Chapter One

Being a Black Girl in the American Academic Institution

"Get an education and they can't take that away from you." ~Minyon Freeman Robinson

Traditionally, public education's lesson content dismissively underrepresents Black students by focusing on Eurocentric people and culture; as a result of this, Black students come to believe that they are not valued. Not only are current lessons devoid of Black cultural experiences, but current instructional pedagogy also has even fewer visible Black female role models and examples of the Black life experience in math, science, social science, and literature . Furthermore, educational research is slow to move in the direction of investigating Black girls' educational development because of the limited frameworks and research agendas that do not recognize the importance of multiple identities, oppressions, and consciousness (Evans-Winters & Esposito, 2010). This is primarily because, historically, Black women were considered useful for breeding and identified as property. Currently, Black girls are socially constructed to depict the opposite of whiteness (Evans-Winters & Esposito, 2010). According to Evans-Winters and Esposito (2010), "Because of racism, sexism, and class oppression in the U.S., [Black] girls are in multiple jeopardy of race, class, and gender exclusion in mainstream educational institutions" (p. 13).

Public education's curricular content reinforces oppressive narratives and adversely impacts Black girls, both academically and behaviorally (Jacobs, 2016; Lane, 2017; Sampson & Garrison-Wade, 2011). Additionally, many Black girls do not get to see positive representation in the school day to refute these negative stereotypes (Boutte, Kelly-Jackson, & Johnson, 2010; Price-Dennis, 2016; Pringle et al., 2012). The problem is that many classroom teachers have not developed skills to create lesson plans and activities inclusive of Black history, culture, and/or the Black experience for Black girls to relate to in their academic experience.

Data collected in 2017 by the National Assessment of Educational Progress (NAEP; "NAEP reading," 2018) reported that 49% of Black fourth-grade students performed below the basic level in reading while 22% of White fourth-grade students performed below the basic level in reading. When students got to the eighth grade, the difference between the two groups remained with 40% of Black students performing below the basic level compared to 16% of White students ("NAEP reading," 2018). A major problem in the public education system is that it lacks and needs to provide instructional pedagogy that honors, builds on, and strengthens Black students' identity and self-efficacy, which endorses Black students to exercise persistence and achieve academic success (Ladson-Billings, 1995). More importantly, educational researchers have begun to acknowledge the need for Black girls to have interventions to support their learning experiences, just like their male counterparts (Lane, 2017).

It is necessary for school leaders to utilize pedagogy and strategies that directly address oppressive instructional bias in the classroom. All students would benefit from curricular content that pushes them to think critically of the oppressive narratives and Eurocentric norms that American culture and society have accepted. Prior research shows that incorporating the culture of the students represented in the classroom as an instructional practice is a means to address oppressive curriculum content and biased teaching practices to become more inclusive (Jacobs, 2016; Lane, 2017; Sampson & Garrison-Wade, 2011). The practice of including culturally related instructional content based on the students in the classroom allows teachers to link academic content to what is already familiar to students as well as gives teachers the ability to face addressing oppression in the curriculum (Boutte et al., 2010).

In a 90-day report, San Francisco Unified School District's superintendent, Vincent Matthews (2017), detailed a well-documented history of Black students as the lowest- performing cultural group via California assessment data. Matthews (2017) reported that in 2016-2017, statewide assessment data showed that 19.3% of Black students throughout SFUSD scored proficient in English language arts compared to 54.5% of all students within the district scoring proficient and 13.4% of Black students tested proficient in math compared to 50.8% of all the students in the district. Additionally, the report stated that in the 2016-2017 school year, 74% of Black students in SFUSD were defined as not meeting grade-level standards in at least one subject. Black students in elementary school reported the lowest percentages across the four domains of cultural-climate; support for learning, fairness of discipline and rules, safety, and sense of belonging; compared to their peers of other ethnicities and the entire district at large. Ultimately, the report depicted an instruction gap that must be addressed to instruct all students adequately and effectively.

The city of San Francisco is framed as America's societal portrait of a free-loving destination for equality filled with liberal men and women. This equality frame needs to be qualified because San Francisco's symbol of equity primarily focuses on gender equity rights and not racial equality. The San Francisco Department of Public Health (SFDPH; 2018) produced a Black/African American Health Report based on the city's Black/African American Health Initiative, which acknowledges economic inequity as an additional reality plaguing the health of the

Black community in the city. The city of San Francisco has now been labeled as the most expensive place to live in the entire world, and Black girls are being raised in a city where, currently and historically, the primary living option is public housing. This is the direct result of policies put in place in the mid -20th century:

> Redistricting public works projects in the 40s and 50s demolished most of the [Black/African American] housing and businesses in the Fillmore area, and many residents moved into public housing developments in Sunnydale, Potrero Hill, and Bayview-Hunters Point. Those concentrations of [Black/African American] communities remain today. (SFDPH, 2018)

This is a crucial concern because many Black women are heading these households as single mothers (United Way, 2015). With these realities for Black girls living in San Francisco, it is crucial for the public education system to address the academic needs of Black girls.

Black Girls Become Black Women

Black girls face challenges that are not limited to their involvement in school, and in many cases, their challenges are compounded later in life into womanhood. This was evinced by Monique Morris (2016) when she addressed the need for separating Black girls from Black students as a whole when it came to creating intervention supports. In her book, *Pushout: The Criminalization of Black Girls in Schools,* Morris reported on the future of Black girls moving into womanhood with data from 2014 that stated 25% of Black women lived in poverty while unemployment for Black women age 20 and over at the end of 2014 was 8.2% compared to 4.4% for White women and 5% for all women. In 2012, Black women earned 89% of what Black men earned and comparatively only 64% of what White men earned. Black women were also disproportionately employed in low wage jobs paying less than $21,412 per year (Morris, 2016). These statistics reflected a possibility for Black girls who are not educated and are not provided with resources to overcome poverty.

The Problem for Our Girls and the Need for Decolonization

Black girl, Black girl, where do you want to learn?

In a space that welcomes my history, culture, and physical attributes as beautiful. In a space where I am affirmed as capable and given tools to fight the oppressive system that embodies the country I call home.

Black girl, Black girl, where do you want to learn?

I want to learn in a classroom with teachers who look like me or, at the very least, teach me about me: my historical roots, my cultural traditions, and how to think beyond my ABCs and 123s.

Simply put, public elementary schools do not provide Black girls with the opportunity to engage in a welcoming learning environment where they find various examples of Black women embedded within their curricular textbooks or readings as well as class assignments (Pringle et al., 2012). This fact alone is a primary factor for disengagement with the academic system for many Black schoolgirls. In addition to Black schoolgirls being disengaged by the curriculum due to their sparse presence within curricular content, many educational leaders—both classroom teachers and school administrators—do not merit advocating for Black schoolgirls in the face of academic oppression. The task of educating Black girls becomes a responsibility left for Black schoolgirls to independently navigate since Black minds have historically been neglected by the American public education system.

Furthermore, Black girls' minds and bodies are subjected to racism and sexism in the media and school policies that directly move to dehumanize Black girls' identities (Evans- Winters & Esposito, 2010). This results in suppression of the Black female voice in the classroom (Boutte et al., 2010; Price-Dennis, 2016; Pringle et al., 2012). As a result, Black female students' chances of being successful in school are reduced because they do not see themselves represented in their academic instruction and are held to a Eurocentric normative standard of behavior (Morris, 2007; Pringle et al., 2012). Because educational leaders are the gatekeepers to information sharing in the classroom and academic promotion, there is a need to develop communication strategies that support Black girls' academic experience to keep them in the classroom; thereby, providing them with access to education that will, in turn, increase academic achievement.

To begin addressing the problem of Black girl's absence from the official curriculum, I created a decolonizing intervention curriculum and program that was implemented at an urban elementary after-school program with a primarily low-income population in the San Francisco Unified School District. This study was a critical action research project based on qualitative grounded theory. The purpose of the intervention was to expose third- through fifth-grade Black girls and girls of color to diverse forms of literacy centered around Black history and culture. This research stemmed from the premise that Black girls flourish in school with consistent exposure to relevant content that allows them to critically form healthy opinions of themselves and allows them to believe that they are intelligent and capable of being academically successful (Lane, 2017). The literacy-based curriculum and program is titled *Queens Gettin' Lit!*, which is positioned to encourage cultural appreciation and bolster academic confidence in the classroom. *Queens Gettin' Lit!* is a step toward honoring "Africentric values" at school while building grade-level literacy skills.

My study used critical action research as a means to improve public elementary education's oppressive instructional content through the omission of Black culture to liberating students through culturally inclusive lessons. This pilot study exposed Black girls and other girls of color to literacy content based on Black history and cultural experiences. Students in this program got an opportunity to learn, develop, and practice analyzing, critiquing, and summarizing skills to complete program projects, which included researching and writing. I documented their experiences, as well as my own, to determine how engagement with this curriculum in such a program impacts both academic achievement and students' views of themselves and as learners.

The San Francisco Unified School District has recognized the need for targeted instructional support to engage Black students. My research further narrowed the focus to Black girls due to the systemic underrepresentation of Black girls' and Black women's experiences historically and currently. The following research questions guided how I conducted the study:

What is the impact on urban Black girls of an after-school intervention program on their (a) cultural heritage knowledge, (b) cultural heritage agency, and (c) academic progress in grades three through five?

The experiences of the pilot study participants and my own reflections were positioned to illuminate the necessity of culturally affirming content in developing self-identity within an academic setting. The participants' engagement with the curriculum, along with my implementation, countered the typical public education experience. Participants ultimately were culturally reaffirmed throughout the duration of the study and were taught content that resembled themselves by an instructor who looked like them.

My aforementioned elementary school experience in the book's introduction is common for Black girls in schools where the majority of the students do not look like them. The majority of my academic experience in first through ninth grade was primarily in White spaces. I was a cultural anomaly that teachers did not know how to address. As an adult educator, I reflect on those experiences and find it hurtful and disrespectful that my teachers did their best to include patriotic activities in the classroom while silencing my voice and pride. I felt like those teachers were intentionally not acknowledging my Black heritage.

Teachers do not have the right to dismiss the students they are responsible for, whether the classroom is composed of a majority or minority of Black students. In schools where the majority of students are not White, and teachers do not look like the students in the classroom, it is the teacher's responsibility to make that classroom feel inclusive of all the people who are represented in the room. Case in point, Black girls' academic experiences are at risk.

Many Black girls have experienced challenges in school based on racially biased perceptions from their teachers and school authority figures (Morris, 2016; Morris, 2017). This study worked to support Black girls' engagement, persistence, and retention while countering instructional practices that reinforced oppressive, normative behavior standards, and expectations that negatively impact Black female students, both academically and behaviorally. Its goal was for Black girls to learn more about their Black culture and history as well as develop cultural pride. Another goal of this study was for school leaders to acknowledge the significance of cultural inclusion in instructional practices and for teachers to use this study to acquire culturally affirming strategies that help them modify their lesson plan content to be less Eurocentric and more intentional about incorporating culturally inclusive, affirming content into instruction. Last, the study promoted education equity by cultivating the development of Black students' identity to refute negative Black stereotypes and biases that enter into public school classrooms. What was learned from this intervention helps educational researchers, leaders, and teachers expand their knowledge on how to prevent Black girls from experiencing alienation in the classroom and enables Black girls to succeed better in school and life.

Chapter Two

Black is Always Beautiful: My Discovery of the American Public Education System

"The most disrespected person in America is the Black woman, the most unprotected person in America is the Black woman, the most neglected person in America is the Black woman." ~El-Hajj Malik El-Shabazz better known as Malcolm X

El-Hajj Malik El-Shabazz, otherwise known as Malcolm X, aptly titled his speech while simultaneously indirectly asking on May 5, 1962: *Who Taught You to Hate Yourself?* His words come from the speech he delivered at the funeral of Ronald Stokes, who was killed by the Los Angeles Police Department. In 2019, Malcolm X's words still ring true.

I propose that the educational research presented in this literature review argued that the American education system is a piece of the answer to the question posed in his speech title. The idealized purpose of school is to impart information and knowledge to students and not isolate students from their learning experience. The American education system mirrors the sentiment of Malcolm X's profound words as it recreates obstacles for many Black girls' academic experiences because of racially biased perceptions from their teachers and educational leaders (Morris, 2007). Furthermore, Black schoolgirls are academically disengaged due in part to a lack of inclusion within instructional content (Pringle et al., 2012). This leads to some Black schoolgirls being identified by terms such *as deficient, struggling, and below grade level* (Price-Dennis, 2016). Black schoolgirls are also pushed out of the classroom because they quickly get labeled as loud, defiant, disrespectful, and angry (Annamma et al., 2016; Morris, 2016). Some teachers are compelled to curtail Black girls' demonstrative behavior and who lack awareness of the value of advocating for their students of color, which includes teaching them about the achievements and life experiences of Black people and culture (Morris, 2007; Pringle et al., 2012).

My research proposes to educational leaders, scholars, teachers, and student advocates that academic spaces must decolonize their instructional practices to become culturally inclusive by intentionally embedding Black history and culture into curricular content. When Black schoolgirls see themselves positively within their learning experiences, they thrive and develop asset-based identities (Jacobs, 2016; Lane, 2017). This dissertation study was also purposed to learn from the experiences and reflections of the pilot study participants and me, the pilot study instructor, who taught the self-written curriculum that refutes negative Black female stereotypes as well as the biases that enter into public school classrooms and disengage student learning.

The literature review presents the case that providing Black schoolgirls with asset-based learning experiences on Black history, culture, and community is at the root of decolonizing the American education system and a step toward improving academic outcomes for Black schoolgirls (Jacobs, 2016; Lane, 2017; Lane, 2018). Decolonization is the liberation of the oppressed mind, which leads to academic progress. This literature review sought to identify instructional practices, pedagogies, and theoretical frameworks at the root of the liberation process, which is also at the heart of decolonizing the Black schoolgirls' mind within the oppressive American education system. The review of relevant research also examines curricula in elementary and high school classrooms that are inclusive of the Black schoolgirl experience and the effects of receiving culturally inclusive curricular content on the academic achievement of Black schoolgirls. The culturally inclusive curriculum is defined as academic lessons that feature or have examples of Black life and/or achievements of Black people in math, science, history, and/or language arts subject content areas.

Scope and Methodology of the Literature Review

A liberated mind breaks the shackles of colonization. For Black schoolgirls to see possibility, hope, and a future to succeed, they must know who they are. It is well documented throughout academic research that there is a significant gap between the academic performance of Black girls and their White peers and peers of color within the American public education system. The omission of Blackness within the American public elementary education curriculum prevents Black elementary schoolgirls the opportunity to learn about their African and American historical past full of cultural traditions. Therefore, Black girls must arm their minds to critically analyze and successfully matriculate through the American public education system. There is a process of simultaneously decolonizing the American public education system and the Black elementary schoolgirl's mind. The following themes presented in this literature are central to my research goals: 1) move toward the liberation of the Black elementary schoolgirl's mind and 2) decolonization of the American education system:

- Black feminist pedagogy (BFP) implemented with culturally responsive critical theory (CRCT) positively impacts cultural identity development,

- Black pride equates to the positive correlation between cultural identity and academic confidence, and

- Implementing Black history and culture within public elementary education instructional content is an act of decolonization.

This review of relevant literature pertaining to school instructional practices includes quantitative, qualitative, and mixed-method studies focused on individual teachers using culturally inclusive instructional content for Black female students as well as focusing on critical pedagogy as a framework for instructional practice. This paper brought attention to the following questions:

1. Does elementary education instructional content give Black girls an opportunity to see positive reflections of themselves and their culture as well as give them a chance to learn about their culture?

2. Are schools implementing curriculum inclusive of Black females' life experiences? If so, how are Black girls being included in the curriculum?

3. What are the student outcomes when Black girls are taught using curricula inclusive of their life experiences?

The following databases were used to complete this review: Academic Search Premier, ERIC, PsycInfo, EBSCO, and GoogleScholar. Keywords used in the search were:*elementary education; Black female students; Black girls; academic achievement; curriculum; African American female students; effects of: curriculum, cultural appreciation, Black girls; African American girls; cultural identity; critical race feminism; Black feminist thought; identity development; cultural appreciation; and after-school programs.* I chose articles from peer- reviewed journals that dated as far back as 2003. I also used branching as a search strategy for finding more references.

Theoretical Framework

Decolonization is a sociopolitical fight. Within this literature review, I argue that there are two decolonization fights occurring in concert with each other: One fight is to liberate Black elementary schoolgirls' minds from the oppressive American public education system, and the other fight is to decolonize the American public education system by including instructional content that affirms Black history and culture in the elementary public education system. Therefore, this theoretical framework utilizes critical race theory (CRT) as the cornerstone for the need to decolonize elementary public education to combat racism within the academic institution. CRT acknowledges that race and racism infiltrate all areas of American society and within American institutions (Solórzano & Yosso, 2002). Metaphorically, CRT is the hole that prepared the foundation upon which my theoretical framework was built. Continuing on with the structure-building metaphor, critical race feminism (CRF) was then applied to the framework as "the concrete" to support the foundation. CRF recognizes that Black girls encounter harmful race and gender sociopolitical forces within academia, so my framework uses CRF as an instrument to promote equity in public elementary education (Evans-Winters & Esposito, 2010). CRT and CRF collaboratively reinforce the framework's argument by establishing the need for decolonization (Evans-Winters & Esposito, 2010; Solórzano & Yosso, 2002). With the foundation established, Black feminist thought (BFT) and CRCT were included in this framework as strategies to liberate Black elementary schoolgirls' minds and public elementary school curricula. Developing a Black woman's schema comes from multiple theoretical approaches. Black elementary schoolgirls benefit from the use of BFT because of its empowerment factor on the mind (Lindsay-Dennis, 2015). Additionally, using CRCT was a practical instructional approach for decolonizing public elementary education (Wiggan & Watson, 2016). Essentially, this theoretical framework provides a blueprint for creating warriors within the social justice battle.

Critical Race Theory

Black girls are excluded from the classroom learning experience because they are not reflected in their instructional content. Black schoolgirls should see positive examples of Black life in their academic content to critically analyze mediums and stereotypes that negatively define them. CRT frames the problem of public school's elementary education curricula as culturally exclusive content that removes Black females and other groups of color from instructional content (Solórzano & Yosso, 2002). In practice, CRT also frames public elementary schools' curricula as problematic by acknowledging and establishing the role race and racism play in the education system while also functioning as a strategy to eliminate racism and other oppressive forms such as bias based on gender, class, and language (Solórzano & Yosso, 2002). CRT provides a social justice focus for the equality and liberation of the oppressed (Solórzano & Yosso, 2002). Using CRT as a framework seeks to identify oppressive biases and stereotypes among school authority and curricular content while analyzing school instructional practices and transforming school leadership and school culture.

Black schoolgirls are being oppressed within their academic experience, even though the education system is meant to liberate them via access to knowledge. CRT's theoretical lens challenges traditional research that explains the experiences of people of color (Solórzano & Yosso, 2002). The CRT framework recognizes as well as legitimizes experiential knowledge, which, in turn, strengthens and validates Black girls' voices (Solórzano & Yosso, 2002). This framework challenges school leaders, teachers, and students, as well as researchers, to examine elementary schools' oppressive curriculum content and develop instructional experiences that are inclusive of the Black female student experience.

In addition to examining the removal of Black female students from academic spaces through the CRT frame, it is important to use intersectionality theory as a framework because Black girls do not experience being Black and female separately (Collins, 1990). Kimberle Crenshaw has been identified as the mother of the term intersectionality. Nonetheless, intersectionality has been a conversation in academia since the 1960s and was birthed from BFT with the women of the Combahee River collective (Taylor, 2017, p. 4). Founder of the collective, Barbara Smith, acknowledged that the women did not term the phrase intersectionality but that the collective expressed the analysis of multiple oppressions strengthens one another to create new classifications of oppression and using that analysis as a blueprint to activism (Taylor, 2017, p. 4, 12). Black feminist theorists understand that as Black women, our life experiences cannot be condensed to race or gender but must be understood on their own terms (Taylor, 2017, p. 2). Black women's identities are steeped in political oppression; therefore, the experiences of Black women must be analyzed differently in academia. According to Taylor (2017), "It is necessary to validate the particular experiences of Black women in our society while also measuring exactly the levels of oppression, inequality, and exploitation experienced in African American communities" (p. 3).

Intersectionality addresses the societal effects of being both Black and female and that the combination of the two plays a role in being pushed out of the classroom (Morris, 2007). It is important to understand and define for Black girls so that they can use Black women's prior shared knowledge and experiences to navigate and anticipate the world (Price-Dennis, 2016). Black girls face a different reality that comes with disadvantages, such as being stereotyped as aggressive and defiant, which other cultures or gendered persons do not face (Morris, 2016). This fact highlights that school administrators and teachers must begin to acknowledge bias and shift its education practice.

Critical Race Feminism

CRF embodies the entire issue of race and gender at the center of the Black woman's struggle (Evans-Winters & Esposito, 2010). Black girls are the lowest on the social agenda totem pole. According to Evans-Winters and Esposito (2010), "Because feminist epistemologies tend to be concerned with the education of White girls and women, and raced-based epistemologies tend to be consumed with the educational barriers negatively affecting Black boys, the educational needs of Black girls have fallen through the cracks."

Therefore, it is necessary for Black girls to engage in identity work (Lane, 2017). CRF frames the decolonization fight of Black girls' minds and the elementary public education system as not a singular fight but a racial fight due to sexism and gender inequality. Furthermore, using a CRF in this study adds to the growing literature that recognizes Black female students need to be studied further through the lens of race and gender.

Black Feminist Thought and Culturally Responsive Critical Theory

BFT is a framework situated under the umbrella of critical pedagogy, which includes CRT that educational and social science researchers use as a framework to give a voice and power to Black girls who are overlooked in classrooms and overly researched without asset-based outcomes (Lane, 2018). This framework also prepares Black girls with vital tools to overcome societal and institutional barriers because it presents "learning strategies informed by Black women's historical experience with race/gender/class bias and the consequences of marginality and isolation" (Omolade, 1993, p. 31). Education is another extension of a racist government institution. To counter current racist-based educational practices that push Black girls further out of educational spaces, BFT can be employed to empower Black girls to persist through these racist spaces. Likewise, education and social science researchers must continue to explore strategies that improve academic outcomes for Black girls in the classroom. Researchers can employ BFT as a tool and resource of analysis for providing agency to Black girls in the classroom and giving Black girls a voice in the research.

The application of BFT into praxis operates as Black Feminist Pedagogy (BFP) for the freedom of all oppressed people and centralizes the oppression of Black women while empowering Black women through activism by placing Black women at the center of the analysis (Lane, 2018). According to Omolade (1993), "Black feminist pedagogy aims to develop a mindset of intellectual inclusion and expansion that stands in contradiction to the Western intellectual tradition of exclusivity and chauvinism" (p. 31). Black girls in American public education benefit from a curriculum that utilizes BFP to challenge academia and society because it is a strategic tool for instructional decolonization and liberation of Black females (Lane, 2018). It is a true form of advocacy and agency for Black girls.

BFT offers a framework for pedagogical practice and an alternative to traditional public education curricula. It is an opportunity for Black girls to engage in counter-narratives that have traditionally placed them in a space of objectification while providing them with hope to write a new story within society and academic institutions (Lane, 2017). BFP also promotes the decolonization curriculum and decolonizing space for community building based on validating culture while giving power and agency to Black girls (Lane, 2017). Public elementary education has the potential to empower Black girls by implementing BFP into curricular activities and projects.

CRCT is a response to the needs of Black girls in public elementary schools because it recognizes that Black girls need a decolonizing curriculum that affirms Black culture. This theory decenters whiteness in the traditional public education curriculum while also critiquing race in school (Wiggan & Watson, 2016). CRCT is another framework used as a strategic tool for decolonizing curricula because it provides resistance to cultural hegemony and promotes "learning about Black history in school resists common exclusionary practices found in traditional schools" (Wiggan & Watson, 2016).

This theoretical framework utilizes the aforementioned theories as a strategic approach to analyzing education research literature to decolonize Black elementary schoolgirls' minds and the American public education system's curricular instruction. CRT and CRF provide insight into the need for decolonization within the American public education system (Evans-Winters & Esposito, 2010; Solórzano & Yosso, 2002). BFT and culturally responsive critical theory are implementation methods for educational leaders and researchers to employ when working directly with Black girls in academic spaces (Lane, 2018; Wiggan & Watson, 2016). BFT supports the cultural identity development of Black girls, while CRCT is the decolonization tool that counters the current Eurocentric learning viewpoint (Lane, 2017; Lane, 2018; Wiggan & Watson, 2016). Therefore, preparing Black girls to resist and critique instructional content while fighting to decolonize the elementary public education system are identified by the following literature review themes:

- Black Feminist Pedagogy implemented with Culturally Responsive Critical Theory positively impacts cultural identity development,

- Black pride equates to the positive correlation between cultural identity and academic confidence, and

- Implementing Black history and culture within public elementary education instructional content as an act of decolonization.

The Fight to Decolonize Public Education

Black girls are represented in the population of students who are removed from classrooms, which contributes to them receiving less access to quality education based on their absence from instructional content (Mendez & Knoff, 2003; Morris, 2016; Wun, 2016). In California alone, more than 30,000 students were referred to law enforcement in the 2009-2010 school year (Wun, 2016). A more recent report published in 2014 from the U.S. Department of Education stated that Black students accounted for 18% of the student population and were 42% of the referrals to law enforcement, 35% of school-based arrests, and 29% of all the students expelled (Wun, 2016). Additionally, Black female students were six times as likely to be suspended or expelled from school in comparison to White female students (Annamma et al., 2016). Zero tolerance policies have allowed schools to rely on law enforcement and school security guards as resources for student discipline (Morris, 2016).

With Black females being banned from classrooms, academic systems are permitting Black female students to be academically alienated and identified as delinquent (Morris, 2016). Nationwide, 48% of Black girls who are expelled do not have access to academic instruction (Morris, 2016). This identity ascription has the potential to perpetuate itself in the life of these Black schoolgirls, in essence, eliminating Black girls from the academic landscape while contributing to their low academic performance (Morris, 2016).

With Black schoolgirls being pushed out of the classroom, there is a need to develop strategies that support their academic experience to keep them in the classroom; thereby, providing them access to education that would, in turn, increase academic achievement. American public elementary education curriculum reinforces racist, oppressive narratives. Furthermore, social norms continue to negatively impact Black female students, both academically and behaviorally.

For Black girls to progress successfully through the public education system, there is a need to resist the current, traditional public elementary education curricular instruction and implement culturally affirming instructional content. Educational leaders are in a position to decolonize instructional, curricular content to engage Black girls in school. This is because curriculum content can effectively be used to develop and impact identity as well as address oppressive narratives and social norms that negatively impact Black schoolgirls within the public education system (Jacobs, 2016; Lane, 2017). Therefore, schools need to address the differential treatment of Black students when it comes to their academic instruction (Paris & Alim, 2014).

Black Feminist Pedagogy Implemented with Culturally Responsive Critical Theory Positively Impacts Cultural Identity Development

America's racist societal underpinnings have created and defined the concept of normalized behavior, which is then defined by one homogenous group: White people (Morris, 2007). American public elementary classrooms and curricula exclude many students who are not considered mainstream (Howard, Patterson, Kinloch, Burkhard, & Randall, 2016). Mainstream defined by society is identified as popular and primarily socially acceptable. Students come into classrooms learning that privilege and "acceptable" behaviors are associated with the White homogenous group (Morris, 2007). As a result, it is imperative that Black girls be exposed to a curriculum that uses a critical lens toward postcolonial and de-colonial concepts to revolutionize current hegemonic practices and perspectives in the classroom (Howard et al., 2016).

Identity also plays a large role in students understanding their own position within their academic experience; consequently, schools are one of the largest influences on the life trajectory of Black girls (Chavous et al., 2003; Morris, 2016). When teachers label Black girls as the loud, disrespectful, and/or the angry contributor in classroom disruption, many of them internalize the role of the troublemaker and feel ostracized by their instructor—reinforcing the disconnected feeling between student and school (Morris, 2016). Curriculum content based in critical relevant pedagogies promotes student learning from a critical conscious perspective because it moves beyond the Eurocentric learning model and attempts to normalize high achievement for Black students (Boutte et al., 2010).

BFT is the alternative curricular framework Black girls benefit from in their academic spaces because it is a "self-defined lens through which Black [girls] can be seen, and their experiences understood in relation to themselves" (Howard et al., 2016, p. 759). BFT also provides Black girls with the ability to experience Blackness in contrast to the monolithic identity typically ascribed to them because BFT acknowledges and appreciates individuality among the African diaspora (Howard et al., 2016). The use and practice of theory is pedagogy. BFP "opens the possibilities for Black women and girls to push back against oppressive forces that seek to limit their forms of agency and self-empowerment" (Howard et al., 2016, p. 759). The implementation of BFP provides a way for Black girls to gain self-knowledge. BFP's intention is placed on uncovering the racial blinders of traditional Eurocentric curriculum places on American history and way of life. BFP can also be strategically used as a decolonization tool in elementary schools by centering elementary public education curriculum on Black girls and rejecting colonizing agendas that are rampant in public education and adopted school curriculum (Howard et al., 2016).

Lane (2017) and Jacobs (2016) studied the integration of BFP into a curriculum design that creates an oppositional space to liberate and challenge oppressive curriculum narratives and depictions of Black females. Monique Lane (2017) studied a group of approximately 20 Black high school females who participated in a literacy group, exposing them to Black feminist literature with BFP and CRF during the students' lunch period over a two-year span. The outcomes from the study showed that students' participation resulted in positive dispositions toward school, and the curriculum provided Black female students with the opportunity to unify around a new definition of the Black woman. Lane's (2017) curriculum implementation is a positive intervention because students reported leaving the program with a stronger appreciation for their own culture and developed positive attitudes toward school. Jacobs (2016) found in her 16-week study of approximately 15 Black high school girls that they took pride and celebrated their identities. Charlotte Jacob (2016) reported on a larger phenomenological study that integrated critical media pedagogy and BFT to develop her curriculum that engaged a group of Black female students to acquire an oppositional gaze at current depictions of Black females. Results from the study propose that a curriculum concentrated on understanding and growing resistance and resilience strategies by evaluating media is a powerful tool for Black female students to form their own understanding of race and gender. Both studies position Black female students as the focus of their studies using curricula that integrated the student participants' identity and the students' experience of being a Black female (Jacobs, 2016; Lane, 2017). As a result, the high school participants had the opportunity to unify around a new definition of Black women and feel positive about school (Jacob, 2016; Lane, 2017).

Wiggan and Watson (2016) took the notion of culturally responsive pedagogy (CRP) and fused together critical theory to produce CRCT. CRP is used to address the cultural differences between teacher and student by adopting the following six characteristics to instructional practice: (a) validating, (b) comprehensive, (c) multidimensional, (d) empowering, (e) transformative, and (f) emancipatory to support home culture and deconstruct racism in schools (Matias & Mackey, 2016; Wiggan & Watson, 2016). Wiggan and Watson (2016) combined critical theory with CRP to decenter whiteness and provide resistance to cultural hegemony while examining the racial inequality in school curricula. Wiggan and Watson designed a K-8 private elementary school study implementing an African-centered curriculum, which can also be identified as a decolonization curriculum. The curriculum involved critical analysis and required reciprocated respect from both students and teachers. The curriculum also recognized students as assets by acknowledging that students come into the classroom with useful skills from their ethnicity, heritage, and culture. This became the basis for effective teaching and positive student-teacher relationships, which are critical for Black students (Wiggan & Watson, 2016). Students reported increased self-esteem, confidence, and pride from learning accurate information about Black history and culture.

Essentially, CRCT affirms students' race and cultural identity while challenging racial inequality in school curricula. Black girls need curricula that resist the current academic structures that are pushing them out (Wiggan & Watson, 2016). Implementation of CRCT can be used as a strategy to decolonize classroom curricula for Black girls to learn and develop critical thinking skills. The additional benefit of using CRCT is that it validates the students and draws on their knowledge as an asset to the classroom (Wiggan & Watson, 2016), as opposed to looking at the students as empty vessels to deposit knowledge into, also known as Paulo Freire's (2000) banking method from the Pedagogy of the Oppressed.

Schools and instructional leaders play important roles in supporting the navigation of cultural identity development (Jacobs,2016). Curriculum designed to concentrate on understanding and developing resistance and resilience strategies is a powerful tool for Black female students to form their own understanding of race and gender (Jacobs, 2016). Culturally inclusive, decolonizing curricular content also gave Black girls the opportunity to rally around a positive Black identity, which allowed these students to feel connected to each other and their academic experience (Lane, 2017). Intentional, culturally inclusive curriculum implementation can also be seen as a positive behavior intervention because students have a stronger appreciation for their own culture and develop a positive attitude toward school (Lane, 2017).

Black Pride Equates to the Positive Correlation Between Cultural Identity and Academic Confidence

There is a connection between cultural understanding and academic performance. While the aforementioned studies discussed building a cultural identity in school through instructional content, Shin (2011) studied the influence of Africentric values, race/ethnicity identity, and community perceptions on academic self-efficacy and found a positive relationship between connectedness to Black culture and academic performance. Black students who transcend stereotypes and societal identities have a developed sense of self that promotes "academic self- efficacy" (Shin, 2011). Culture plays an important role in Black students' academic behavior, and schools should take notice and develop programs that honor "Africentric values" (Shin, 2011). This is because racial identity largely determines the relationship with academic achievement (Cokley, McClain, Jones, & Johnson, 2011). The results of this study also provide a context for schools to utilize community resource partners that are effectively executing Africentric cultural practices.

Black schoolgirls flourish with consistency and exposure to instructional content that allows them to (a) critically form healthy opinions of themselves, (b) believe that they are intelligent, and (c) believe that they are capable of being academically successful (Lane, 2017). Having a solid, positive understanding of self produces pride. Group pride is connected with positive school feelings and perceptions of being academically successful (Chavous et al., 2003). Therefore, school leaders must create a decolonized, inclusionary culture where students' identities are acknowledged and validated for Black students to operate freely in their belief of themselves being productive and smart (Khalifa, 2010).

Black girls with a strong appreciation for Black culture exhibit academic confidence (Lane, 2017; Shin, 2011). Black schoolgirls who do not identify with societal standards of the Black female conduct themselves with a new sense of identity (Jacobs, 2016). With this new identity comes a new sense of confidence that translates into an ability to overcome obstacles in their academic performance (Shin, 2011). This body of research confirms that when Black girls have the opportunity to negate oppressive societal norms through exposure to non-traditional critical pedagogy, then they are able to develop racial identity and are willing and want to be academically successful (Cokley et al., 2011; Jacobs, 2016; Lane, 2017; Sampson & Garrison- Wade, 2011; Shin, 2011).

Armed with Black pride, which can also be identified as having a greater knowledge of self and defined as cultural identity, Black schoolgirls push themselves to do well in school (Jacobs, 2016; Lane, 2017). The depicted studies provide evidence of Black female students succeeding when teachers of color help Black female students navigate and construct racial identity using CRCT through academic instruction (Jacobs, 2016; Lane, 2017; Sampson & Garrison-Wade, 2011; Wiggan and Watson, 2016).

There are also educational researchers who have reviewed literature about Black students gaining Black pride as potentially damaging (Zirkel & Johnson, 2016). Zirkel and Johnson (2016) reviewed educational research studies conceptualizing Black racial identity in education. These educational researchers are noteworthy because they present research within the body of the reviewed literature that holds an opposing view on the political act of decolonization in public educational spaces. Zirkel and Johnson (2016) recognized the growing literature within the social sciences regarding the positive connections between Black identity and academic performance. Their work also pointed out research that remains in the literature suggesting, "perhaps a strong, positive Black identity is 'dangerous,' distracting Black youth and even their peers away from school and academic accomplishment" (p. 301). Furthermore, their research pointed out that social science literature continues to misidentify the concept of Blackness and Black pride as anti-White and redefining whiteness as the norm. The notion of Black pride, as a negative concept, is not an idea to which this study ascribes to. Cultural identity arms Black girls with resilience and is a tool of racial discrimination resistance, which promotes academic success (Zirkel & Johnson, 2016). Lane (2018) contended cultural congruence is a critical explanation for the high levels of academic success and engagement of elementary school-aged African American students. Nyachae (2016) concluded that it is important for intervention programs with a target population of Black girls to consider using an empowering curriculum that embodies a culturally affirming identity context.

Implementing Black History and Culture and Critical Pedagogy within Public Elementary Education Instructional Content as an Act of Decolonization

Schools must counter the reproduction of negative Black female stereotypes by establishing transformational space to develop racial identity (Jacobs, 2016). The examples of decolonization curriculum integration in these studies depict Black female students' ability to develop personal connections to school through critical identity development coursework with an instructor who has taken a personal interest in the development of the students (Lane, 2017; Jacobs 2016). It is important for school leaders and classroom teachers to develop opportunities for Black schoolgirls to develop a racial identity outside of societal definitions using critical pedagogy for students to understand themselves as well as connect to their academic setting (Chavous et al., 2003).

Lane (2017) and Jacobs (2016) illustrated studies that (a) exhibited instructional content developing a racial identity and (b) provided instructional context promoting critical thinking skill development for students that mirrors rigorous academic instruction. With the help of teacher and authority figures, school curriculum content, and peer interactions, Black female students are explicitly and implicitly developing their identity in schools. Because of this, the school curriculum can help navigate how Black females understand themselves (Cokley et al., 2011; Jacobs, 2016).

The research suggests that Black girls be allowed to dispel oppressive societal norms and sharpen their critical thinking skills through critical analysis and examination in school (Jacobs, 2016; Lane, 2017). This approach allows Black female children not only to see themselves in their learning content, but it allows them to develop necessary critical thinking skills that cross all content areas. Critical pedagogy is a strategy in the practice of decolonization curriculum, which also allows Black girls to develop a critical consciousness that challenges the neutrality of curricular content and helps to define a new identity for themselves (Boutte et al., 2010; Price-Dennis, 2016). These young ladies become armed with knowledge and skills that transform their way of thinking about themselves and the way they move through society. Black girls no longer feel connected to the negative imagery and subscriptions that formerly labeled them; they redefine themselves as well as believe in themselves (Cokley et al., 2011; Jacobs, 2106). Therefore, schools that implement critical analysis into their instruction promote a sense of self -worth for Black female students as they develop their identity and begin to appreciate their culture (Jacobs, 2016; Lane, 2017). When Black female students develop a sense of pride and belief, research reports an increase in academic identification and achievement (Cokley et al., 2011).

In addition to the use of Critical Pedagogy (CP) in education and social science research literature, Culturally Responsive Pedagogy (CRP) is also present in the research as an instructional means to develop skills that build race identity. CRP gives teachers a chance to connect academic content to what is already familiar to students as well as give teachers the ability to face addressing oppression in the curriculum (Boutte et al., 2010). Sampson and Garrison-Wade (2011) studied students' proclivity for culturally relevant lessons embedded with CRT versus standard subject content lessons at a Colorado high school. Students reported a preference for seamless integration of culturally relevant content into their regular curriculum because the lessons were highly engaging. The use of lessons with culturally relevant themes means that there is a heightened importance for teachers and students to be able to openly discuss difficult topics honestly and be ready to navigate through bias and stereotypes. Teachers should also use CRP to position themselves to learn from their students and not just about their students (Boutte et al., 2010).

Decolonization ignites political change, which potentially results in resistance and pushback. Opposing research has argued that strong connections to Black identity are dangerous (Zirkel & Johnson, 2016). That is to say that learning about one's self—one's essence—is a distraction from academics and academic progress (Zirkel & Johnson, 2016). These same educators, academics, and social science researchers theorized and normalized Eurocentric cultural norms as anti-Black behavior, promoting the alignment of the idea that Black students obtain success by adopting what is identified as White, academic, behavioral norms (Zirkel & Johnson, 2016). The idea that promoting positive Black identity is determined to be dangerous is the reason for the revolutionary political pushback to decolonize curriculum in public elementary education.

These researchers have gained traction with the notion that Black youth incur negative outcomes when taught to have a strong, positive Black identity (Zirkel & Johnson 2016). As a result, Black girls do not have the luxury of being a product of the American public education system. The American public elementary education system is comprised of racism and White supremacy, making it most necessary for white people to move beyond their own deficit, racist, biased thoughts to interpret Black students as exhibiting cultural pride and not diminish their pride (Johnson & Zirkel, 2016).

Black elementary girls' public education learning experiences require allies from people of all backgrounds for Black schoolgirls to succeed (Zirkel & Johnson, 2016; Pringle et al., 2012). It is important for educational leaders to support the inclusion of Black history and culture within instructional content (Jacobs, 2016; Lane, 2017). Ultimately, the decolonization of the American public education system is a unifying act of educational justice for all students of color.

Conclusion

There is a need to develop strategies that support Black elementary girls' academic experience to keep them in the classroom; thereby, providing them access to education, which will, in turn, increase academic achievement. I argue that oppressive classroom social norms and reinforcing oppressive narratives through the racist American public elementary education curriculum continue to negatively impact Black schoolgirls both academically and behaviorally. Instead, elementary school teachers need to modify their practice and incorporate decolonizing, culturally inclusive curricular content into their instruction. This leads to Black girls refuting the negative Black female stereotypes that enter into elementary school classrooms and increases Black female academic achievement.

The review of relevant literature did not have many studies based in public elementary education. Of the numerous studies searched, two highlighted grades below middle school, starting in third grade. Moreover, traditional public elementary education structures and resources do not provide Black girls with an opportunity to see themselves. This results in Black women educators choosing to develop decolonizing curriculum and strategies for Black girls as an intervention to racist academic school day programs. These educators were also researchers working outside of their regular school hours based on their commitment and personal stake in Black girls. Not only are these educators and educational researchers, but they are also social justice activists directly addressing oppressive practices in school through culturally relevant school leadership based in CRT and CRP, primarily in high school settings. Public education school leaders can and must begin to decolonize the practice of elementary education and challenge social injustice while seeing Black school girls as assets in the classroom.

The literature presents a gap within this body of research in regard to the use of non- Black teachers implementing these curricular pedagogies on developing cultural identity. The literature would benefit from exploring how non-teachers of color can teach the same culturally relevant lessons to determine if non-teachers of color can produce the same positive outcomes. Since the education system has a majority of non-Black teachers to see a greater impact on increasing Black female students' academic achievement, non-teachers of color need to be trained about how to implement racial identity discussions through critical pedagogy.

There is also a lack of research literature that positions Black female students' voices at the center of the analysis. Future research would benefit from including a detailed account of the perceptions of Black female students on their academic experience concerning their lived experience (Cokley et al., 2011). The literature would also benefit from including the belief systems of Black female students and seek to understand how their lived experiences coupled with their belief system, help them to manage and navigate their academic development (Chavous et al., 2003).

This review of the research primarily focused on the needs of middle and high school Black girls by infusing critical pedagogies into the academic curriculum. However, educational researchers must also engage in studies of Black girls in their young developmental ages while they are in elementary school. Identity development occurs over a significant amount of time at crucial child development stages. This review of relevant literature showed the need for more qualitative research centering on Black female elementary school students to understand how factors such as race, culture, and community connect with their ability to develop a cultural identity as well as academic lives (Shin, 2011).

Schools must incorporate the use of critical pedagogies to address the differential treatment of students of color as well as acknowledge the change in the treatment of students of color when culture shifts (Paris & Alim, 2014). Furthermore, all students would benefit from curricular content that pushed them to think critically of the oppressive narratives and norms that American public elementary education, culture, and society have accepted. Most importantly, to keep Black school girls in schools, they must be able to see themselves positively reflected in their academic experience.

CHAPTER THREE

DEBUNKING WHITE SUPREMACY THROUGH DECOLONIZATION

"Take the first step in faith. You don't have to see the whole staircase, just take the first step." ~Dr. Martin Luther King, Jr.

Methodological Approach: Case Study

The purpose of my study is two-fold 1) to service an urban public elementary school community with an after school literacy based curriculum for third through fifth grade Black schoolgirls which supports decolonizing the minds of Black school girls by providing them with an opportunity to develop their self-esteem, cultural identity, and agency through culturally relevant content and 2) to gather data on how urban public elementary Black schoolgirls interact with the decolonizing aspects of the *Queens Gettin' Lit!* curriculum in relation to their academic experiences. My research question is an inquiry into Black schoolgirls' academic experiences and how those experiences contribute to their cultural appreciation, cultural agency, and academic progress: *What is the impact on urban Black girls in grades 3-5 of an after school intervention program on their a) cultural appreciation, b) cultural agency, and c) academic progress?*

I chose case study as my methodological approach to sharing the researched information to intentionally add elementary Black schoolgirls' voices into the education research literature. This approach also allows the audience to learn more from and gain an understanding of urban Black elementary schoolgirls. There is a growing body of academic research that discusses intervention programs and activities that support cultural identity development (Burkard, Howard, Kinloch, Patterson, & Randall, 2016; Evans-Winters 2007; Lane 2017; Lane 2018; Nyachae 2016; Wiggan & Watson 2016). Many of those researchers also chose to share the voices of the researched students; however, there were no studies that included elementary students (Howard et al 2016; Lane 2017; Lane 2018; Nyachae 2016; Wiggan & Watson 2016). Therefore, my research works to fill the elementary school perspective void within the body of relevant research as well as aligns with my theoretical framework that Black girls and women are rarely the drivers of research of and for us.

The case study approach gives space for the effects of the tested intervention to be shared from the voices of the participants. It provides a picture of how the students received and interpreted the activities. Additionally, the participants' own discussions demonstrate the utility of the program and curriculum for the purpose of decolonizing the minds of Black schoolgirls.

I used the grounded theory approach for coding all pre- and post-intervention interviews along with participants' words and artifacts from the curriculum's activities. All the interviews and video blogs were transcribed and I coded the text for reoccurring words and ideas that developed into emergent themes. Along with the case study participants' interviews and student work, the whole group participant interview and the in-session circle discussions were transcribed and coded for reoccurring themes as well. I wrote holistic memos from my curriculum facilitation reflections and used grounded theory coding for reoccurring emergent themes.

This study inquires about the impacts of the tested curriculum for the following outcomes: cultural heritage knowledge, cultural heritage agency, and academic progress. During the implementation of the curriculum, participants freely shared their ideas on the aforementioned research inquiry themes. Session discussions, reflection blogs, and activities and projects were collected as data evidence from student participants. As the curriculum implementer, I wrote post-program implementation reflections notes, which in addition to providing data for the research study will be used to develop a facilitators' guide for future implementation.

Queens Gettin' Lit! The Decolonizing Intervention

Queens Gettin' Lit! is a twelve week literacy pilot program for Black girls who attended an urban public elementary school in San Francisco. The program met twice a week for an hour after school for 12 weeks. The instructional content was based on weekly themes that focused on Black history, the Black community, Black culture, and self. This curriculum also targeted supporting third through fifth grade students developing critical and higher order thinking skills. The curriculum was designed with the goal of inspiring and motivating a community of Black girls by facilitating self-esteem, cultural identity development, and agency through literature, dialogue, and positive interactions with their peers and women of color.

This pilot study sought to address the needs of Black girls who may have experienced challenges matriculating through school and attaining academic progress due to instructional content not being relevant to their own lives which could have the potential to disengage them from learning (Pringle, Brkich, Adams, West-Olatunii, & Archer-Banks, 2012). Each week students completed projects based on the unit's theme. Students had an opportunity to learn, develop, and practice analyzing and summarizing skills in order to complete program projects, which included researching and writing. The goal of the curriculum was to initiate knowledge of self through starting with an exploration into historical African royalty to develop the foundational understanding of the Black experience in America by moving into the historical experiences of Black culture by examining the slave trade, civil rights movement, and social justice activism.

Queens Gettin' Lit! Theory of Action: Educate to Liberate

Students participating in the 12 week curriculum engaged in content that countered the dominating cultural narrative of Black females. The curriculum draws from the following theories to decolonize the public education system and the minds of Black elementary school girls: Critical Race Theory, Black Feminist Thought, and Critical Race Feminism. These theoretical frameworks acknowledge and establish the role racism and sexism play out in American society and American institutions. As students read and learned about African history, they engaged in activities purposed to develop written language and vocabulary skills. Using Critical Race Theory, Black Feminist Thought, and Critical Race Feminism as theoretical frameworks for the curriculum allows the students to learn how to critique mainstream mediums as well as learn more about themselves.

I anticipated that participants would develop connections to their cultural identity which equates to a feeling of pride and that participants would develop their critical thinking skills in order to analyze content related to identity, culture, and history. I base these assumptions on two particular studies by Lane (2017) and Sampson and Garrison-Wade (2010) where both studies implemented curriculum with students using Critical Race Feminism and Critical Race Theory as their framework. Lane (2017) researched Black girls and engaged the participants in critical race feminism through her own curriculum, which resulted in students reconstructing their identity definition of Black femininity. Her findings also showed that participants used their voice for being change agents at the school site. Research participants from Lane (2017) engaged in curricular content reflective of the participants' culture using Critical Race Feminism that cultivated agency and ethnic identity.

Sampson and Garrison-Wade (2010) researched a high school history course and implemented curriculum using critical race theory. The researchers work highlights that students' standard school experiences should include cultural connection to learning. Sampson and Garrison-Wade (2010) found that students feel valued in academic spaces when instructional content reflects the lives and histories of Black students. Participants from the study acknowledged that the curriculum fostered a connection between themselves and the instructor due to the nature of the content being discussed; as a result, student participants reported a desire to have more coursework using a Critical Race Theory lens (Sampson & Garrison-Wade, 2010).

The Future Queens: Participants' Background Information

The *Queens Getting'* Lit! pilot study was designed for approximately 15 third through fifth grade Black girl participants who were enrolled in a partner organization's elementary after school program. The partner organization's after school program is held at an urban public school with a predominantly Black and low socioeconomic demographic where over 80% of the student population receive free and/or reduced meals. *Queens Gettin' Lit!* is a voluntary after school curricular program situated within the existing after school program at the partner elementary school. All participating students were research study participants, and thus recruitment involved making clear to parents and students the dual intervention/research purpose of the project. Participation in the program was completely voluntary and after the regular instructional day. Parents who did not wish for their child to participate in the study simply chose not to sign up.

Recruitment for the study involved providing information to potential participating families in two contexts. First, I introduced myself to the school community at the beginning of the school year at events like Back-to-School Night and briefly explained the program. Second, I hosted my own program orientation session to provide more details and confirm voluntary participation in the study. The teachers of the community had already welcomed the pilot program and were simultaneously working to recruit participants for the success of the pilot's launch.

To maintain confidentiality throughout the duration of the study, I stored all content obtained from the course of the study in a locked mobile filing storage bin as well as used pseudonyms for all participants. Out of the fifteen total participants in the pilot study, I have decided to highlight three participants within this case study analysis. The participants remain anonymous because they are depicted using pseudonyms.

Future Queen 1

Kiara Jackson was a third grade student. She participated in the majority of *Queens Gettin' Lit!* sessions being present for 77% of the pilot study. Many days Kiara came into session ready and willing to participate in the planned activities and discussions.

Future Queen 2

Diamond Hearns was a third grader at the after school program. Diamond attended a majority of the pilot study as well and was present for 73% of the pilot's duration. She also came to program regularly with a willing attitude and open spirit.

Future Queen 3

Nikkia Edwards was a fourth grader. She participated in 41% of the pilot study. Nikkia engaged in most of the program discussions and activities with mild resistance.

Researcher Positionality

My positionality as the researcher is also one of an employee within the same school district. At the start of the pilot study implementation, I was promoted to the role of an administrator at a different school site. For the duration of the study, I served as curriculum instructor for

Queens Gettin' Lit! thus positioning me in the role of teacher/ researcher. As a Black woman, this positionality allowed me to develop relationships with the students and analyze how the intervention unfolded through an "insider" perspective. Because many Black girls experience classrooms led by white women, Lane (2017) and Jacobs (2016) both acknowledge that being Black women researchers influenced the shape of their studies because students have an opportunity to connect with a teacher of the same ethnicity. This perspective informs my research conceptualization, implementation, and analysis.

Data Sources

The case studies reflect data collected before, within and after the intervention to create a full story of participants' experiences. These include: 1) participants' student work, termed participants' artifacts; 2) participants' reflections, which were shared through written reflections and video blogs; 3) participants' session discussions and pre-/post-interviews, which have been transcribed for this study; and 4) my own reflections as the researcher and curriculum facilitator.

Participants' Artifacts

Student participants engaged in unit themed projects and assignments. Student work includes poetry, notes from documentaries, reflections and writing assignments as well as savings boxes, self-affirmation posters, and vision boards. The student work also known as participants' artifacts were created throughout the pilot study serves as a primary data source.

Throughout the intervention term, student participants responded to prompts in their own reflection journals. During each session meeting, students were prompted to respond to topics based unit themes. Towards the latter part of the study, students responded to prompts using video and began video blogging their responses. The content collected in the participants' journals and video blogs serve as a primary data source for the study.

Participant Interviews and Whole Group Discussions

Upon entering and exiting the program, participants were interviewed 1-on-1 and participated in a final whole group interview. The individual interviews and group interview were recorded on audio files stored on my password protected personal laptop. All participants were interviewed 1-on-1 approximately one month prior to the start of the intervention. Interviews were held at the elementary school during after school program hours in an unoccupied classroom. Interviews were designed to capture participants' responses to questions regarding their elementary school experience. Through the duration of the program, circle discussions were held on various topics related to the research question. These circle discussions provided a space for participants to share their thoughts and ideas freely. A final whole group interview was held at the end of the program for student participants to share reflections of their *Queens Gettin' Lit!* experience. Individual 1-on-1 interviews were conducted again in the same manner at the conclusion of the program. The transcriptions from the in-session circle discussions, pre-/post- interviews, and final whole group interview serve as my final primary data source.

Researcher/Curriculum Developer and Facilitator Reflections

In addition to the student participants' reflections of the curriculum and program, my reflections as curriculum facilitator were included as a participant reflection. As the pilot study facilitator, my perspective gives the dissertation research the instructor's challenges and victories throughout curriculum implementation. My curriculum developer's reflections provide a look into the experience of testing decolonization content on elementary schoolgirls.

Analysis

This is a grounded theory qualitative study presented as a narrative case study. Using grounded theory, I am analyzing all data using coding cycles and memos. The participants' artifacts and reflections were coded for insights into students' self-esteem, cultural identity, and cultural agency. The interviews and whole group transcriptions are coded noting similar and recurring topics and/or patterns from the participants.

I selected focal students for the case studies, once the data set was complete; in order to choose representative participants for whom sufficient data existed. It was also important for the research to reflect the experiences of the grade levels represented; therefore, I have third and fourth grade students presented in the narrative case study analysis. In addition to the collected data sources, my research includes participants whose academic performance levels range from high to low performing based on the Fountas and Pinnell literacy assessments. The final narrative case study criterion was the participants' attendance rate must be at a core or periphery level. A core participant is a research study participant who attended 60% or more of the pilot study program. A periphery participant is a research study participant who attended between 59%-20% of the pilot study program.

CHAPTER FOUR

BLACK QUEENS IN THE MAKING

"Identity helps you to understand your purpose." ~*Bishop Christopher Carl Smith*

Be the change you want to see in the world. All day. That is the essence of *Queens Gettin' Lit!* In order for young Black girls to see themselves as the change they want to be in the world they must know who they are. The essence of knowing yourself comes from an informed position of knowing and understanding your own history: the origin of self. *Queens Gettin' Lit!* exposes young Black girls to a cultural history and knowledge that connects them to their cultural identity roots. The curricular content consists of activities purposed to develop critical thinking skills. Black history and culture and critical thinking skills are not taught regularly in public elementary language arts classrooms.

Queens Gettin' Lit! The Dissertation Research Pilot Study

The *Queens Gettin' Lit!* dissertation pilot research study was launched within a predominantly low socio-economic neighborhood of San Francisco. The school is primarily composed of Black students along with Pacific Islander, Latin American, and Southeast Asian and Asian students to complete the total student of color demographic population. A non-profit after school program hosted the implementation of the *Queens Gettin' Lit!* research study and the implementation of the study was funded by another local non-profit organization positioned to support the ideas of San Francisco Unified School District teachers. The curriculum implementation analysis of *Queens Gettin' Lit!* originates from the following data sources, as discussed in Chapter 3: participants' artifacts, in-session circle discussions, whole group participants' interview, participants' reflections, pre/post participation interviews, and researcher/curriculum facilitator's reflections.

Given the situating of this program in a voluntary after school program, attendance was often irregular and impacted data collection. Tables 4.1, 4.2, and 4.3 summarize attendance of participants.

Table 4.1 Grade Levels of *Queens Gettin' Lit!* Pilot Study Participants

Grade Levels of Queens Gettin' Lit! Pilot Study Participants	
Grade Level	**Number of Participants**
Third Grade (3rd)	7
Fourth Grade (4th)	7
Fifth Grade (5th)	1
Total Number of Pilot Study Participants: 15	

Table 4.2 *Queens Gettin' Lit!* Pilot Study's Participation Zone of Proximity

Queens Gettin' Lit! Pilot Study's Participation Zone of Proximity		
Program Participation (%)	**Participation Proximity Zone**	**Number of Participants**
Research study participants attended 60% or more of the pilot study program	Core Participants	7
Research study participants attended between 59%-20% of the pilot study program	Periphery Participants	4
Research study participants attended below 20% of the pilot study program	Outlier Participants	4
Total Number of Pilot Study Participants: 15		

Table 4.3 Queens Gettin' Lit! Pilot Study Session Attendance

Queens Gettin' Lit! Pilot Study Session Attendance	
Session Number and Date	**Session Attendance out of the Total Number of Pilot Study Participants (%)**
Session 1: 11/26/18	67%

Session 2: 11/28/18	67%
Session 3: 12/3/18	53%
Session 4: 12/5/18	56%
Session 5: 12/12/18	33%
Session 6: 12/17/18	50%
Session 7: 1/7/19	47%
Session 8: 1/9/19	63%
Session 9: 1/14/19	67%
Session 10: 1/16/19	47%
Session 11: 1/23/19	40%
Session 12: 1/28/19	53%
Session 13: 1/30/19	73%
Session 14: 2/4/19	40%
Session 15: 2/6/19	40%
Session 16: 2/11/19	27%
Session 17: 2/13/19	27%
Session 18: 2/20/19	53%
Session 19: 2/27/19	53%
Session 20: 3/4/19	33%

Session 21: 3/6/19	56%
Session 22: 3/11/19	53%

Curriculum Content Creator's Reflection on Decolonization Curriculum Implementation

I had a dual role in this research project as researcher and curriculum developer/facilitator. As the curriculum developer/facilitator of Queens Gettin' Lit!, I would debrief my facilitation experience at the end of each session. The debriefs included my feelings toward the teaching experience, my assessment of the participation from session activities, and reflections of my interactions with the participants and the curriculum. I analyzed my debrief reflections using a grounded theory approach coding for recurring themes. I also wrote holistic memos after session debriefs.

Intended Research Goals

As the developer of *Queens Getting' Lit!*, I began the intervention with clear ideas regarding the purpose and anticipated outcomes. *Queens Gettin' Lit!* was designed to be a decolonization curriculum and intervention program purposed to counter the mis-education of Black girls' minds. The curriculum teaches historical facts on African history and Black American history as well as culture. The curriculum's content interjects imagery via historical videos and pictures of Black American women who were powerful and silenced, murdered, and criminalized. Participants learned about Black women who flourished, were successful and created our current day progress. The curriculum presents information to elementary school girls to develop a seed of knowledge for young girls to learn their cultural heritage origins from the African continent where they ruled as royalty. The curriculum's content exposed participants' minds to untaught cultural heritage and taught the elementary school participants that they too can grow into the same women they learned about coming out of the continent of Africa and here in America.

Queens Gettin' Lit!'s purpose is to expose Black schoolgirls to knowledge regarding the Black woman's transition from royalty into oppression and the fight for liberation. The curriculum focuses on moving through time from Africa to North America and illustrates examples of Black women's resilience as well as provides examples of Black women who fought against white supremacy in a country that taught Black people to hate themselves: the United States of America. Participants were exposed to Black women within the curriculum who strategically fought for humanity and to be acknowledged by a government and a country that pilfered African people from within the continent. Participants were taught an accurate depiction of Black history which included teaching them that Africans built the foundation of the American economy and were then banished and relegated out of power in the Reconstruction Era in order to keep Black people in an oppressive government and education system.

Reflections on Implementation

Participants entered into the *Queens Gettin' Lit!* space with hesitancy towards doing traditional school assignments in the intervention program; specifically writing. Students did not want to write in their program provided journals yet they loved their notebooks. Writing was not a chore for the girls because they did not have ideas. Writing was a difficulty because many of the girls lacked the confidence in their writing skills and ability to communicate in writing.

As curriculum developer and facilitator, I was especially excited about the idea of launching *Queens Gettin' Lit!* I noticed hills and valleys that arose during the first half of the program prior to the winter recess for student participation. I coded my post session holistic reflection memos from the initial roll out of the program, which included teaching units 1-3, and the following are the recurring themes from those memos:

Disengagement

On December 3, 2018, I taught the third session on A Stolen Nation and two students checked out of the activity completely. On this particular day, two students were picked up by family members early which left me with five students remaining in program. From the five students, three participants were actively researching the topics for the day (MAAFA also known as the Black Holocaust and the Trans-Atlantic Slave Trade) on iPads using Bing.com and Ask.com. The level of disengagement occurred on two levels: 1) students getting removed from the program and 2) students checking out of the program session's activity. On one level, many of the participants' family members were picking up students prior to the session ending, which made it difficult for students to fully connect to the content. I spoke with the director of the organization to adjust the timing of the *Queens Gettin' Lit!* program but the schedule could not be changed. The director recommended that I initiate family engagement strategies to get participants more connected to the program. Subsequently, I did reach out and connected with some families in order to keep students in the program for the full hour; however, participation remained up and down throughout the entire study.

The next level of disengagement came from the participants telling me that they were not having fun doing the session activities I had planned. As the facilitator, I was concerned that the participants were not enjoying their experience in the program. The activities I had planned were academic and reminiscent of a regular school day lesson activity; so I revamped the second half of the curriculum when we returned from winter recess.

On December 12, 2018, I facilitated session five on Wise Queens: Leading Ladies (Part 1) and recognized that some of the participants' disengagement came from session topics themselves. For example, I launched *Queens Gettin' Lit!* with content on African royalty and historical facts about women from the continent of Africa prior to enslavement, then we discussed enslavement and moved into the Civil Rights Movement. "The vibe of the girls is dry because the first half of *Queens Gettin' Lit!* is Black history [primarily in America]." As a result, some students fully disengaged from the program by refusing to attend this day's session. "Many of them just said oh I don't want to go [to program] because I don't want to." This was one of my lowest sessions attended with 33% participants present. The students' physical disengagement response was a major message to me that I needed to change my implementation strategy and come up with activities that were fun and did not remind them of a regular school day. I inquired with the participants inside and outside of *Queens Gettin' Lit!* sessions to understand how I could improve the quality of the program's instructional content. Many of the girls made it clear to me that they wanted to have fun. When I asked them more specific questions on what would make the experience more fun, participants had difficulty sharing ideas that would improve session activities. For example, one participant told me, "We just want to have fun" and when I asked what that looked like she responded with, "I don't know." By the end of the first half of implementation, I was disappointed that participation numbers had dropped but I had a plan to revise the curriculum over the winter break and return with activities the girls would enjoy.

Receptive Learning

While I did experience participants' disengagement, I also had a core group of girls attending sessions regularly who were being taught and exposed to new concepts. During one of the sessions, the students' primary activity was to engage in online research as digital scholars. I was proud of these participants because they were receptive to learning how to digitally research information using search engines they were unfamiliar with. Participants shared that they discovered new information about the slave trade in addition to learning the new name for the slave trade, MAAFA also known as the Black Holocaust.

Participants were also receptive to their learning experience during a different unit session since the activity for the day involved coloring images of Black women leaders and watching mini documentaries on Assata Shakur and Dorothy Height. "I had a solid five girls. They really rocked. They watched the video intently. They were listening. They were learning. They were telling me how they enjoyed going home and sharing the information with their moms" (post-implementation reflection debrief). At this point in the scope of the curriculum, the content was moving into social justice and activism. Students were finding their way in the program as I was finding mine as curriculum developer and facilitator.

Queens Gettin' Lit! Post Study Reflections

Because these themes represented opposing concepts, I grew introspective as I reflected on my own teaching practice. I recognized that disengagement could have come from my own lack of clarity on the program itself. Many of the participants were not fully aware of what *Queens Gettin' Lit!* offered and what was expected from them as members of the program. Therefore, as I continue to improve, I will clearly explain to students the expectations and objectives of the program in a student and parent orientation session. I see the importance of having the students involved with the parent(s) and/or guardian(s) at the onset of the program. I also realized the importance of providing students with a unit overview description along with unit objectives at the beginning of the session prior to session activities.

Instructional Practice and Instructional Content Goals

As a veteran teacher, I totally recognize the importance of providing information prior to exposing students to new content. Time management became a challenge while executing this pilot study due to circumstances outside of my control such as starting the program on time with all the participants present. This was because many of the study participants were involved in other programs in addition to

Queens Gettin' Lit! that conflicted with the *Queens Gettin' Lit!* program time and so many days I found myself diving directly into the activity in order to collect student work data.

Evidenced in my holistic reflection memos, I found keeping the students engaged a challenge in addition to relaying the importance of ensuring participants remain in the intervention for the entire length of the program to families. In the midst of these challenges, I did experience success with the girls because they learned new information about African queens and new skills such as using the Internet for online research. With these experiences, I continued to implement *Queens Gettin' Lit!* and recognized that I was going to have to make changes during the upcoming Winter Recess to return in 2019 with more exciting, engaging content for the students.

Modifications to Respond to Student Interest

In 2019, I modified and adapted the curriculum's expectations to reduce the tension and elevate creativity. Queens Gettin' Lit!'s curriculum promoted Black pride, exploration and wonderment into Black history, culture, community, and self. The girls interacted with activities focusing on the aforementioned areas and shared their ideas and thoughts on video known as a video blog. The idea of the video blog came from the students' resistance to journal writing. In order to continue to use writing as a tool, I did not totally eliminate writing from the implementation of curriculum; however, writing was no longer the expected journaling product. Instead, participants shared their reflections through video. This provided an opportunity for me to see growth in the participants' comprehension of the content as well as see the development of the participants' personal reflections over time.

Through the implementation of this curriculum, I recognized the fallacy in the way public education expects students to produce outputs in order to determine understanding and define success , which is evidenced in my January 28, 2019 reflection memo:

"When asking students to think about creating at school, our students are so used to thinking one way about what a classroom can look like and feel like... But I wanted them to think more creatively. So I was trying to really push their thinking creatively and overall I think that is it's difficult because they haven't had an opportunity to do so.

Forcing our teachers and the education system to move beyond traditional expectations and activities will help Black girls. [This is] because ultimately what I've been able to witness over these past few weeks are girls wanting to be a part of something bigger than themselves as a collective while being exposed to new information in a way that's creative and doesn't keep them bound in a seat, at a table, or confined to a writing assignment ."

By the end of the intervention, participants were still requesting to learn more about African queens and I recognized that transitioning to slavery from African queens takes the empowerment out of learning Black history and comparatively is like taking the wind out of the participants' sails.

Final Participant Research Reflections

It's hard work being a black girl. For many Black girls, school is boring. School is not about work for them. All children must go to school, many children continue to come regularly because they enjoy socializing with their peers, and some are coming to school because they enjoy learning. Essentially my participants are still children who wanted to have fun and should be treated as such especially outside of the school day.

I recognized as the instructor that I was going to have to change my own belief systems about teaching racial identity to engage my after school intervention program participants. For example, I had believed that slavery was an important topic to teach in the identity development arc of a Black woman; however, that is the primary education Black girls receive in school regarding their cultural identity. Therefore, they have a thorough understanding of slavery and do not require additional education on the subject.

I specifically had a student tell me that we don't need to learn about Black history because they were already taught information on slavery. The participants explained to me that their school was named after a former slave and their truth resonated with me. It was then when I knew that I would have to eliminate the slavery unit from the curriculum. *Queens Gettin' Lit!* is not intended to replicate the same traditional learning expectations for Black girls that have been forced on them since the beginning of their academic experience. In our final whole group interview, the girls shared that they wanted to learn and be exposed to their culture. The participants also acknowledged that *Queens Gettin' Lit!* was a space for fun, laughter, getting to know each other while being able to do projects and share personal thoughts and feelings.

A Dream Turned Reality

Queens Gettin' Lit! transformed us all. I had the pleasure of creating and teaching content that I have had a desire to share ever since I was an elementary school girl. The intervention's curriculum content was inspired by the lack of Black history and culture being taught in American public education elementary schools. As the case studies depict, all three participants showed growth in the focal areas of cultural heritage appreciation, cultural heritage agency, and academic progress. Additionally, out of the fifteen these three girls developed self-identity, self-confidence, and agency as well as recognized community developed in the space from our consistent gatherings.

CHAPTER FIVE

QUEENS GETTIN' LIT! NARRATIVE CASE STUDIES

"Educating the mind without educating the heart is no education at all."
~Aristotle

From fifteen to three. At the start of the pilot study, attendance was inconsistent. Nine out of the fifteen students were present for pre-intervention interviews. In an effort to get as many students as possible for pre-intervention interviews, I came to the site consistently for two weeks and unfortunately still was unable to interview all fifteen participants. Over the course of intervention study, participation remained inconsistent. At the conclusion of the pilot study, I was able to interview ten out of the fifteen participants. I collected a total of seven pre- and post- intervention interviews from the fifteen pilot study participants, which consisted of four third grade students and three fourth grade students. This interview data became my initial criterion for determining my narrative case study participants.

I selected three narrative case study participants from both grade levels represented out of the seven pilot study participants with interview data on file. Two of the three case study participants are third grade students and were selected because of their high attendance rate throughout the course of the pilot study. I selected one high performing third grade student, Diamond Hearns, and one low performing third grade student, Kiara Jackson, in order to present analysis data from participants who have a broad range of academic ability and skill. I also selected Kiara Jackson because she experienced bullying outside of the pilot study during the school day by a fellow Queens Gettin' Lit! participant. Details of this experience are shared in her case study narrative. Out of the three fourth grade students, one student was a core participant who presented academic challenges and has an Individual Education Plan, another student was present for 20% of the pilot study, and the last student ranked academically proficient via school assessment data and was present for 41% of the pilot study due to conflicts with other after school program activities in her schedule. Therefore, I selected Nikkia Edwards as third case study participant who was present for 41% of the study.

My research question asks: *What is the impact on 3rd-5th grade urban Black girls of an after school intervention program on their a) cultural heritage knowledge, b) cultural heritage agency, and c) academic progress in grades three through five?* This question identifies three focal areas for analysis based on the implementation of the decolonization curriculum: cultural heritage knowledge, cultural heritage agency, and academic progress. Cultural heritage knowledge is defined as having found value and understanding of one's own geographical origin, which includes traditions and customs. Cultural heritage agency is defined by the ability and desire to share information on one's own geographical origin which includes traditions, customs, and historical facts. Academic progress is defined as demonstration of scholastic growth and/or development.

Diamond Hearns

Diamond is a third grade student who has attended Booker T. Washington Elementary School since Kindergarten. A native of the school's neighborhood, Diamond was one of the first students I met on site when I started visiting the campus prior to the launch of the intervention program in the 2018-2019 school year. Diamond was present at Back-to-School night and introduced herself to me along with her mother when I tabled the event for girls to share their interest in *Queens Gettin' Lit!* and for me to share information about the program with the community. She was in attendance at Session One: Royalty, and maintained a high attendance rate for the duration of the intervention program, which classifies her as a core participant. A core participant is defined as being present for 60% or more of the intervention program. Diamond was present for 73% of *Queens Gettin' Lit!*

Diamond is a young lady full of energy and excitement. She is pleasant to be around and helpful. During our Back-to-School night encounter, she repeatedly came to my table to inquire about the details of the pilot study intervention program and reviewed many of the books I had on display that evening. She also brought many of her friends to my table to garner interest from her peers in *Queens Gettin' Lit!* Our next meeting was at our pre-intervention interview where I learned that she was thriving academically and was able to confirm via her classroom teacher that her English Language Arts reading level per the Fountas and Pinnell curriculum and assessment was at an independent level M and instructional level N, which equates to end of the year second grade and beginning of the year third grade reading level.

Diamond secured her placement in the program by returning her family consent form and acquiring an incentive notebook with a young Black girl graduate on the cover in full gown, cap, and diploma at hand. She was a proud recipient of the notebook and returned week after week to participate in the *Queens Gettin' Lit!* pilot study intervention program. The intervention program ended in March 2019 and our time and work together concluded with a final interview. The table below depicts the analysis themes that arose from analyzing the data collected through the pilot study implementation.

Diamond Hearns' Data Analysis Themes	
Research Question Focal Areas	**Core Analysis Themes**
• Cultural Heritage Knowledge • Cultural Heritage Agency • Academic Progress	• Agency • Self-Confidence

Diamond Hearn's data analysis themes include research question focal areas--cultural heritage knowledge, cultural heritage agency, and academic progress--and core analysis themes --agency and self-confidence. A core reoccurring analysis theme is defined as occurring within the analysis five or more times. The following narrative analysis comes from research question focal areas, core reoccurring analysis themes, as well as from the pre-intervention interview, intervention, and/or post-intervention interview:

Cultural Heritage Agency and Knowledge

During the pre-intervention interview, Diamond made it clear that she had no issues with speaking to her teacher about including Black history and culture into the classroom when she stated, "I will ask her and say could we do some project about Black people?" During the intervention program, Diamond stated in her video blog that she would like to be a "college teacher…So I would be a teacher that teach all kinds of students and give them homework about Black people" (Unit 6, Session 12). Lastly, she shared in her post-intervention interview,"… I'm telling [people] about who I am and if [people] don't know a lot about Black people, well, I can tell them." It is evidenced by Diamond's own words that she embodies cultural heritage agency. She also shared an appreciation for her acquired cultural heritage knowledge in our post-intervention interview when she stated, *"[Queens Gettin' Lit!]* been fun because we did fun activities about queens and our culture."

Academic Progress

Diamond came into the intervention program with academic confidence. "I'm proud of me going... high in levels by reading M's, N's, and O's" (Pre-Intervention Interview). Booker T. Washington Elementary School uses the Fountas and Pinnell language arts curriculum and assessment system. In the aforementioned quote, Diamond shares her reading level "M's, N's, and O's", which situates her at the end of second grade to middle of the year third grade. At the end of the intervention, Diamond's reading level was at an independent P and instructional R which means she performs at an end of the year third grade beginning of the year fourth grade level. As the labels imply, independent reading level means that the student is able to read the text and demonstrate comprehension of the text without support while the instructional reading level means that the student is able to read most of the text without support and demonstrates limited comprehension of the text without support. She also demonstrated academic progress when she was able to accomplish her academic goal and shared with me in her post-intervention interview, "I got on the honor roll".

Agency

During our pre-intervention interview, Diamond did not make statements that clearly brought up the theme of agency. Nonetheless, as Diamond experienced the intervention program she began showing her sense of agency immediately with statements such as, "You can always be a hero and girls can always be heroes. You can do what you want... girls can be whatever they want to be" (Unit 4, Session 7).

To have agency means that a person has a sense of understanding and ownership of self to then be a voice for a cause. Diamond experienced *Queens Gettin' Lit!* and began expressing the following: "Girls can also save the world and do what they wanna do and speak if they want. Another thing we need to change is boys getting paid more than girls because girls work really hard with less money" (Unit 4, Session 7; Unit 4, Session 8). Diamond demonstrated her leadership with the following bold statement: "I wanna change all the rules and I wanna be responsible and I wanna be like Donald Trump but I would be way nicer and respect and I will respect others just how I want to be treated" (Unit 5, Session 9). She knows her worth and recognizes that she has the ability to lead in the highest office of the land and do it with more respect than she sees currently demonstrated, by using the superlative – er when describing herself in comparison to this current administration. She goes on to say, "And I would change the policy...I would change the law to like Black people and girls can be whatever they want when they grow up" (Unit 5, Session 9). On a different day in another exercise she states in her video blog, "And I'ma be nice to others and tell a lot of people if they're by homeless people feed them..." (Unit 5, Session 9).

Diamond and many girls like her who participated in the intervention program were exposed to historical and current events presented to them from the lens of a Black woman. Therefore, the intervention content provided a space for free thinking in relationship to community, activism, and improvement. Diamond says, "If I were to be leader of my school, I would tell the kids if the kids wasn't being respectful and responsible...I would tell them to be a leader and be respectful and responsible and nice and I would be one of the leaders and that's it" (Unit 5, Session 10). On other session days she shared in her video blog, "Yes, you can be to all the Black girls out there. You can be who want to be, do what you wanna do, see what you wanna see. So when you grow up, you can do what you wanna do see what you wanna see and be what you wanna be and you can be all the things you want to be and intelligent....be beautiful, smart, intelligent and be yourself" (Unit 6, Session 11; Unit 6, Session 12).

Diamond's presence throughout the *Queens Gettin' Lit!* experience remained consistent. Being an agent of change, Diamond embodied leadership --which is another characteristic of agency --by sharing authentic and candid messages through her video blogs. The following excerpts are from subsequent video blogs during her involvement in the intervention program: "[I] would…make sure that they be a leader when they get into some trouble and to be a follower" (Unit 6, Session 12). "Take care of yourself. Be yourself. Love yourself" (Unit 7, Session 14). "I think [beauty] means be yourself and you can think if you're cute or whatever…I also think [beauty] means cute adorable and be yourself" (Unit 7, Session 14). Diamond concluded her experience sharing the following:

> Dr. Dee: "What was your favorite Queens Gettin' Lit! activity and why?"
>
> Diamond: "…the vision board. Because I can remember all the things I said I wanted to do and I can…and it will remind me what to do."

This statement embodies agency because she is prepared to execute the personal vision for her life as she uses the vision board to remind herself of the plan.

Self-Confidence

Diamond came to the QGL! intervention program with self-confidence evidenced in her pre-intervention interview statement, "[Being a Black girl] means that…when I grow up I can be anything I want anything or any person." Throughout the intervention, Diamond shared self-confident statements to her "viewers" through her video blogs such as:

"We are beautiful!" (Unit 5, Session 9)

"I wanna change all the rules and I wanna be responsible and I wanna be like Donald Trump but I would be way nicer and respect and I will respect others just how I want to be treated…And I would change the

policy like and I would change the law to like Black people and girls can be whatever they want when they grow up." (Unit 5, Session 9)

"If I were to be leader of my school, I would tell the kids if the kids wasn't being respectful and responsible…I would tell them to be a leader and be respectful and responsible and nice and I would be one of the leaders and that's it." (Unit 5, Session 10)

"I am a queen. Queens you can be. You are a queen…I'm a queen and I'm Black and I'm proud. I am a beautiful. I am a queen." (Unit 6, Session 11)

"Roses are red violets are blue we queens and so are you." (Unit 6, Session 13)

By the end of the intervention program, her authentic self-confidence remained in tact evidenced in her post-intervention interview:

Dr. Dee: "Do you like yourself?"

Diamond: "Yes…because I be me. Like when somebody tells you to be someone else and you say no I wanna be myself."

Diamond also recognized the importance of education when she shared via her video blogs: "Just don't forget always go to college and be smart and do what you wanna do and be great to all the Black girls out there" (Unit 6, Session 11). During Session 12, students were prompted to imagine themselves as teachers and Diamond promoted academic confidence when she said, "I want [my class] to be smart so when they got to college they will already know what to do…" (Unit 6, Session 12). It is also interesting that Diamond carries the idea that students are to come to college already knowing instead of considering college as a place where you go to learn and receive information.

Impacts of Decolonization Curriculum

The word queen evokes nobility, strength, and ruler. Diamond's video blog testimonials exude the aforementioned attributes of a queen as well as leadership. For example, Diamond stated she would become a college teacher or the president of the United States. Although she came to the program with agency, Queens Gettin' Lit! exposed her to Black history and cultural facts as well as provided her with a space to share her ideas and explore her creativity and imagination relative to Black history, culture, community and self. Diamond ended the program with the following sentiment, *"[Queens Gettin' Lit!] been fun because we did fun activities about queens and our culture"* (Post-Intervention Interview).

Kiara Jackson

Kiara Jackson participated in *Queens Gettin' Lit!* from the beginning of the program to the end. She was one of the core participants, as she participated in over 70 percent of the program. Kiara is a lifelong resident of an adjacent neighborhood and transferred to the school in third grade. She started her academic path in a dual immersion program at a nearby neighborhood school, Benjamin Banneker Elementary School. At the end of her second grade year her family recognized that she had some very strong challenges with literacy in both Spanish and English. As a result, the family transferred her to her current elementary school, Booker T. Washington.

Kiara Jackson was a new student to Booker T. Washington Elementary School. She had an older cousin, Destiny Jones, in the fourth grade who was also a *Queens Gettin' Lit!* participant. I met Kiara at the beginning of the school year. She was consistently one of the last students to be picked up at the end of the school day. It was on one of those days where she and her cousin were the last students to get picked up from the after school program and the family member signed her participation consent form.

I interviewed her soon after the consent forms were signed. It was in the Fall of 2018 where we had our next encounter in the form of my pre-intervention interview. What followed was a series of *Queens*

Gettin' Lit! sessions, which exposed Kiara to Black history, culture, and community. At the conclusion of implementation, I interviewed Kiara Jackson for a final time in March 2019. The table below depicts the analysis themes that arose after analyzing the data collected through the pilot study implementation.

Kiara Jackson's Data Analysis Themes		
Research Question Focal Areas	**Core Analysis Themes**	**Periphery Analysis Themes**
• Cultural Heritage Knowledge • Cultural Heritage Agency • Academic Progress	• Self-Identity • Self-Confidence	• Community

Kiara Jackson's data analysis themes include research question focal areas --cultural heritage knowledge, cultural heritage agency, and academic progress --as well as core analysis themes --self- identity and self-confidence --and community as the periphery analysis theme. A core reoccurring analysis theme is defined as occurring within the analysis five or more times. A periphery reoccurring analysis theme is defined as occurring within the analysis two to four times. The following narrative analysis comes from research question focal areas, core and periphery reoccurring analysis themes, as well as from the pre-intervention interview, intervention, and/or post-intervention interview:

Cultural Heritage Knowledge

Kiara came to the intervention with a sense of cultural knowledge. She shared her experience with Black History at her previous school stating:

"Black history was fun at my old school cause we had like this party at Black History. Like every Black History. Every holiday. Like every Halloween. We have a party. Every Black History. Like everything, what we do is fun…Like we eat something. We do some projects of Black History. Because like during school and after school we eat and stuff cause we just take a break for doing all the things we could play we can do some art if you want to with your own writing book."

She clearly enjoyed playing and celebrating through parties but did not state that she learned any factual cultural heritage information. Upon leaving the intervention experience, Kiara shares in her exit interview:

"What I learned about Black people is that back in the day, queens got stolen and [white people] became racist…[Coretta Scott King and Martin Luther King, Jr.] did the right thing to make it fair to Black people and white people but sometimes it's kind of still racism…I learned about Black people because in my class we learned about Black people that did the right thing like Madam C.J. Walker, Martin Luther King, Coretta Scott King, Muhammad Ali."

When talking about Black History, now Kiara talks about factual information and she has learned about Black history and does not limit her description of Black History to just about fun and celebrations.

Cultural Heritage Agency

Kiara shared a personal depiction of cultural heritage agency through her idea that being a Black girl is freedom."…Black girls could be anything that they want to be and why because I really don't know. But I'm gonna like try as I can and because I have to be a Black girl is kind of fun…"(Post-intervention Interview). In this description, "to be anything you want to be" is freedom. There's a moment of questioning herself and she recognizes that she doesn't know why Black girls can be free but she is still going to try and at the end of the day, being a Black girl is fun.

There is a need and purpose to separate the two forms of agency. Cultural heritage agency relates to being a conduit of change as it relates to Black cultural heritage versus being a positive agent of change beyond culture. Throughout her time in the program, Kiara acquired a sense of agency as evidenced in her statement, "…girls change the world…" (Unit 4, Session 8). She also states, "Queens should change the world… Queens need to fix the world…" (Unit 7, Session 16). Kiara's statements recognize the importance of queens in the community and the fact that queens are change agents within our community.

Academic Progress

At the beginning of her third grade school year, Kiara demonstrated English Language Arts proficiency of a first grader. This school uses the Fountas and Pinnell literacy assessment program, and at the time of our intervention, Kiara placed at an independent level G and instructional level I, which is a middle of the school year first grade reading level. As the labels imply, independent reading level means that the student is able to read the text and demonstrate comprehension of the text without support while the instructional reading level means that the student is able to read most of the text without support and demonstrates limited comprehension of the text without support.

Kiara initially exhibited a lack of phonemic awareness skills, which are primarily taught in kindergarten and first grade. She did not develop phonemic awareness skills in those foundational grade levels because she was enrolled in another school's Spanish Dual Immersion program. During her primary years, Kiara was taught in a language that was not her first language and went home unable to develop Spanish writing and reading skills. At the start of third grade Kiara demonstrated first grade literacy skills. Her first grade literacy skills showed that she had basic phonics knowledge with poor writing and grammatical structure. This is not to say that Kiara is not a hard working student; quite the contrary, she excelled in producing quality content.

Kiara came to the intervention program with a favorable disposition towards academics and learning: "I like my learning. I like my life…my favorite thing is like reading, playing with other kids, like having groups, having spend-the-nights, and having clubs and stuff. That's my thing" (Pre-Intervention Interview). She goes on to admit that she "kind of" likes going to school "Because people cussing…cusses in class. They bad in this classroom. I just want to make this classroom work so they can like be good and change their actions." (Pre-Intervention Interview). It is evident that Kiara has a personal desire to improve her classroom's learning environment to promote learning.

At the conclusion of the intervention, Kiara depicts academic confidence in her statement, "I describe myself as kind, smart, and bold" (Post-Intervention Interview). She has also now states, "I love going to school but sometimes I'm absent" (Post-Intervention Interview). Here, she acknowledges that she does not attend school consistently by stating she's absent while admitting that she loves being in school. She goes on to say , "…I'm trying to mind my own job. I'm trying my hardest to pay attention" (Post-Intervention Interview).

Self-Identity

The pre-intervention interview was my first encounter with this student. Therefore, it is understandable that the student wanted to share positive behavioral adjectives. "I'm quiet. I'm calm…" (Pre-Intervention Interview). Kiara Jackson used words that present a model student. As is typical with young children that want to please adults by evoking words that depict a non-trouble maker: quiet and calm.

During the intervention Kiara evidenced coming into knowledge of self by stating, "I don't like. I don't know what I was a queen" (Unit 6, Session 11). This statement presents recognition of the fact she was uninformed of her cultural heritage. The word queen has been coded as a connection to identity. As a result, these statements also reflect Kiara missing out on information that links her to her own identity. "I didn't know I was a pretty queen" (Unit 6, Session 11). Kiara originally had no knowledge of her African royalty heritage. Because she did not have this prior knowledge, Kiara's statement depicts an awakening of identity. The idea that she was a pretty queen was foreign and she did not like that she was unknowledgeable about her history.

During one of the intervention activities, students engaged in creating affirmation posters. It was during this activity where Kiara acknowledges self-love and acceptance. "I really, really want to be a better person when I get older. And I want to be a great person when I grow up...I will always love to be who I am" (Unit 6, Session 11; Unit 7, Session 14). Kiara's statements of a desire for self-improvement and to make an impact in the world by stating she wants to be a "great person when I grow up" are strong statements that move far beyond her initial self descriptors: quiet and calm. This statement also recognizes that she loves whoever she becomes, which is a bold statement acknowledging to always possess self-love.

"I think what beauty means is that you're like you...I think it means that you're...happy about yourself and I think it means actually like respect myself...I think that it also means that you can always talk about yourself and it's actually great" (Unit 7, Session 14). Here Kiara shares an authentic definition of beauty that includes self-respect and references internal personality traits/characteristics such as "you're like you" and "happy about yourself and respect myself." Over the course of the intervention, Kiara Jackson took onus of her identity and acknowledged that she in fact embodies royalty: "I am a queen and I treat myself like a queen. Queens don't like to be unfair...I'm a queen. I care about myself and I respect myself." (Unit 7, Session 16; Unit 7, Session 18). Her self-worth and value have been actualized while she defines the role of queen through the lens of fairness.

The last four units of the Queens Gettin' Lit! curriculum is purposed to have students take a more introspective look at themselves since the previous units focused on informative content about African queens, slaves, and Civil Rights leaders. Kiara engaged in activities that focused on the significance of Black women and girls at similar ages who are actively working to improve the quality of life and society's image of the Black community. She was also exposed to information in *Unit 7: Love Thy Self* which focused on valuing the beauty of Black skin color and all of its shades as well as hair texture.

Midway through the intervention Kiara shared, "I love that I can do what I what could can do and what I should do" (Unit 7, Session 18). Kiara is confident in loving her actions and knowing the possibilities of what she can do. There is possibility in this statement and she is thinking about her future while saying she loves this about herself. At the conclusion of the intervention, Kiara stated with confidence, "I describe myself as kind, smart, and bold" (Post-Intervention Interview). She has come to know who she is.

Self-Confidence

Various activities throughout the interventions have encouraged this particular student and is evidenced through her statements like "I am a queen and I treat myself like a queen" (Unit 7, Session 16). There is confidence in the statement. There is no coincidence that many of her testimonial self-confident statements mirror the same self-identity themed statements. Self-identity and self-confidence are not synonymous; however, the fact that Kiara has developed confidence along with her understanding of her identity throughout the intervention process should be noted.

During our post-intervention interview, Kiara demonstrates self-love and positive self-talk in her answer, "Yes! I do. I love myself!...like if I say something negative about myself, I always will believe in myself that...that's not true...I keep saying that and saying that and saying until I'm happy." Her response is encouraging because she is sharing positive healthy behaviors for mental health and self care. Lastly, she is leaving the program self motivated, "I'm proud of myself because I work so hard" (Post Intervention Interview).

Community and Safe Space

Kiara presents as a student wanting to be in school and learn because she favors learning activities and being with friends doing activities in a social setting. She stated in her pre-intervention interview, "… my favorite thing is like reading, playing with other kids, like having groups, having spend-the-nights, and having clubs and stuff. That's my thing…Because it makes me feel better…Like when I'm having a bad day, I can make friends." Ultimately, she ended the intervention program with the following sentiment: *"Queens Gettin' Lit!* …is like a place that you should learn about all Black people and queens and stuff. [We]…learned about queens that lived a long time ago and some of them were still alive…" (Post-Intervention Interview).

Kiara's experience presents another outcome that did not come directly from the curriculum but from the space and the relationship developed in the space. Community was developed and grounded in those day-to-day, week-to-week sessions. Every time she came into the room, she lit up. She was happy to be there. She fed off the energy of the other girls and she was a light in the space. It was at the end of one particular session, when I noticed her light was dim and I knew something was wrong. I inquired and that's when she told me that she was being bullied.

A fellow classmate, who called herself a friend, had bullied her. The girl had written a note and put it in Kiara's desk. The note had an unpleasant, threatening image of her. The little girl who drew the picture laughed and admitted she wrote the note as a joke. Kiara did think the note was funny. Due to the serious nature of the situation, I shared the occurrence with the after school program director and Kiara's classroom teacher. I also communicated with the mother of the student who drew the image because she was a member of *Queens Gettin' Lit!* to explain how the safety of our space had been jeopardized. The level of community we had established had been breached and, as the organizer, I took a stand and temporarily suspended that participant from the program. I did this in order to ensure Kiara's safety and progress. She was thriving in the program and I wanted that to continue for her within the *Queens Gettin' Lit!* space.

Kiara told me, her intervention program teacher, about the bullying incident but did not tell her regular school day teacher. When I asked Kiara why she didn't tell her school day teacher, she said that there was too much going on in her classroom during the school day. Kiara did not feel like the teacher would be able to help support her need because of the other multitude of issues that were arising. As a result, my case study student perceived her regular school day teacher as unable to help her. Of course, I reassured her that any time a student needs help a teacher would listen. But her perception of her teacher not being available for her presented silence in a moment in space and time where she needed an advocate. Therefore, Queens Getting Lit! was able to provide that space and sense of community in order for Kiara to get that information out. Kiara Jackson's needs were addressed by the school community because she felt safe to share when she believed her safety and life was in harm. *Queens Gettin' Lit!* provided a safe space that bred community and a sisterhood, which allowed for her to share sensitive information that she had been holding in her body all school day. The community this program created can be considered a sense of refuge.

Impacts of Decolonization Curriculum

Public education curriculum in America does not educate children on factual occurrences that include Black history and culture in elementary schools. Students get an opportunity to gain a better understanding of American history, which includes Black History as they matriculate much later in the academic institutional journey. Queens Gettin' Lit!

provided Kiara Jackson with the opportunity to see positive imagery of Black history, culture, and community within curriculum units like: Unit 3: Civil Rights and Social Justice, Unit 4: Social Justice and Activism, while moving into Unit 5: She Is Me, and Unit 6: "Queening". The information Kiara shared about her identity changed in her post-intervention interview. By the end of Queens Gettin' Lit! Kiara identified herself as kind, smart, and bold. Post-implementation, Kiara identifies herself using attributes or qualities that demonstrate strong characteristics within her identity as opposed to being calm and quiet. I propose that Kiara used calm and quiet to describe herself because she believed she was supposed to see herself as such because Black girls are told and conditioned to be docile in classrooms (E. Morris, 2007). Kiara knew she was smart. Queens Gettin' Lit! was a space where she was affirmed publicly, consistently, and authentically with love, understanding, and compassion. Queens Gettin Lit! was also a space where she was getting fed knowledge about herself to develop an understanding of herself.

Kiara's student work, reflections, and interviews demonstrate progress in self-identity development in addition to cultural identity development. By developing an appreciation for Black culture and operating in cultural agency Kiara learned to love herself. She stated this in her February 20, 2019 video blog: "I am a queen and my future is that I love that I do what I can do what I should do. I love my features and you are a queen."

Nikkia Edwards

Nikkia Edwards participated in *Queens Gettin' Lit!* from the beginning of the program to the end. She was one of the periphery participants, which means she participated in 41% of the program. Nikkia is a local resident and has been attending Booker T. Washington Elementary School since Kindergarten. This year she was in the fourth grade. Booker T. Washington Elementary uses the Fountas and Pinnell literacy assessment program, and at the time of our intervention, Nikkia placed at an independent level R and instructional level S, which is a middle of the school year fourth grade reading level. As the labels imply, independent reading level means that the student is able to read the text and demonstrate comprehension of the text without support while the instructional reading level means that the student is able to read most of the text without support and demonstrates limited comprehension of the text without support.

I met Nikkia and her mother, Alicia, at the Back-to-School Night event I tabled to introduce *Queens Gettin' Lit!* in the school community. Her mother shared a lot of excitement with me as she explained that Nikkia's an avid reader and would thoroughly enjoy the program since our activities were literacy based. Once Alicia returned the participation consent form, I interviewed Nikkia shortly thereafter. At the conclusion of implementation, I interviewed Nikkia Edwards for a final time in March 2019. The table below depicts the analysis themes that arose from analyzing the data collected through the pilot study implementation.

Nikkia Edwards Data Analysis Themes		
Research Question Focal Areas	Core Analysis Themes	Periphery Analysis Themes
• Cultural Heritage Knowledge • Cultural Heritage Agency • Academic Progress	• Self-Identity • Self-Confidence	• Community

Nikkia Edwards' data analysis themes include research question focal areas --cultural heritage knowledge, cultural heritage agency, and academic progress --as well as core analysis themes --self- identity and self-confidence --and community as the periphery analysis theme. A core reoccurring analysis theme is defined as occurring within the analysis five or more times. A periphery reoccurring analysis theme is defined as occurring within the analysis two to four times. The following narrative analysis comes from research question focal areas, core and periphery reoccurring analysis themes, as well as from the pre-intervention interview, intervention, and/or post-intervention interview:

Cultural Heritage Knowledge

Nikkia Edwards understood self-expression and knew Black historical facts prior to the intervention program. As she shared the following in our pre-intervention interview:

"I'm proud of what I do. I like to dance. Because, I feel like when I dance, it's just the way I'm expressing myself."

"I learned that Harriet Tubman was traded when she was younger and that she ran away from her second slave owner and was put back with her first slave owner and she grew up and got a husband and told him that she was gonna run away and he said if she ever did he's gonna tell her slave master and she helped people get to freedom. Rosa Parks sat on the front of the bus so that Black people could sit on the front of the bus and back in the old days there was more exceptions for whites instead of Blacks."

"...white people are treated with more care than Black people."

The aforementioned quotes are a testament to her ability to retell cultural heritage facts. She was also connected to cultural heritage prior to the intervention as she shared about being a black girl from the continent of Africa:

"Cause I know I'm West African and I know that we make beads and jewelry, masks, weapons. I know they celebrate when somebody has come to visit, when a baby is born and they play the drums and they celebrate for a new chief and that the king of a tribe in Africa always has two feathers" (Pre-Intervention Interview).

Post-intervention, Nikkia continued to demonstrate understanding and pride in being a Black girl from the continent of Africa in her statement:

"I feel like we should study like more about like why Black people were forced to come here...I feel like we should study...why we have certain type of people do certain type of things for our Black people rights because they believe that it was true that we should have the same rights as white people not because we're a different color..." (Post-Intervention Interview).

Nikkia is developing a greater understanding of her place in the Black community and gaining perspective about her place within the larger historical narrative. She also recognized the impact of the intervention program during her exit interview in the following statements:

"The experience has been wonderful. It has made me feel like I can open up to even more people and not like if I meet somebody else like I don't have to be shy doing it... I'm learning about Black history. I want to learn more about [Black history] and like the girls that was also in the program feel like they can learn more on Black about Black history because of what they learn they like liked it and I liked it."

"My favorite activity of Queens Gettin' Lit! is when we got to learn about the queens because like we learned about how bold and how strong they was. How like they just went into war against other people but they were men...[Black queens] was just winning war because it was like just because you're a man and like you're not our color or just because you're a man period don't mean that you're stronger than me because I am Black."

"I'm Black and I'm a woman... I'm strong too like you just can't think that you're stronger than me because there's a possibility that somewhere deep down inside of me I have a strength that is your weakness ...."

Nikkia stated that her favorite activity was learning about the African queens prior to enslavement which came from Unit 1 and our second session together. This is not surprising since Black girls do not get an opportunity to learn historical information before African enslavement in school.

Cultural Heritage Agency and Agency

Within Nikkia's pre-intervention interview, it was clear to me that she was an agent of change. Nikkia entered into the intervention with confidence, agency, and a positive self image. Here she stated the meaning of being a Black girl:

"…being a Black girl means I get to have an open mind and a voice and I get to tell people what I think and I don't think and what I like and what I dislike and that I could stand up to what I think is wrong and help people make changes in the world and the world be a better place" (Pre-Intervention Interview).

She also shared an eagerness to introduce cultural heritage into the classroom when she said, "Yes…I'll ask my teacher like could we do something like go home and do a project based on our DNA" (Pre-Intervention interview). During the intervention she demonstrated that she possessed the ability to speak up for herself as well as change the world around her when she stated the following in a video blog from Unit 3, Session 6:

"Something that like I want to change in like the environment and the first thing is weapons. I feel like guns and stuff should not even be made anymore. If I can change something in my environment and where I live, I'd say no guns allowed and whoever makes another gun would have to go to jail and if somebody sells it also have to go to jail."

"Something that I also wish could change in our environment is that people should give Black people their equal rights and that is my honest opinion cause I am Black and I see a lot of white police officers shoot a lot of Black kids and some kids go outside and play with Nerf guns and it looks like a real gun and people tell the police and the police accidentally shoots the kids."

"I feel like all Black girls should be treated equally and that no boys should judge them just because of the way the look or just because of their gender. Stand up for other people and stand up for what you think is right. Use your voice to let people know that you also have opinions."

By the end of the intervention program Nikkia states, "I like to jump rope because when I jump rope I can beat my own personal record. I like to draw cause when I draw I feel like I can use any colors and those colors could describe my feelings. I like to write poems because I believe that poems are strong."

There is agency in her authentic and self-determined and depiction. Her statement draws on the significance of self-expression through drawing and writing poems as well as acknowledges self-expression as a release of inner feelings and ability to share strength with the world. Nikkia also recognizes the need to educate other Black children on Black history and culture because her own peers are disrespectful to Black kids when she stated:

"just because you're a color or like you're a different race or you're different from somebody else or like you look different doesn't mean that you need to be treated differently [you] should be treated with the same type of rights because you're both human beings like you're both living [beings]. I'm comfortable talking about [Black history and/or culture] because you have a lot of Black kids here who like are like just in general Black kids who like still get talked to that these days by kids that are not their race because of like they're not the same...so [the kids that are not Black] feel like they can just talk to people any old kind of way which is not nice" (Post-Intervention Interview).

Academic Progress

Nikkia entered into the intervention program with a desire to do well academically and had a history of academic achievement. I learned this when she stated, "I have a chance to win the honor roll again this year" (Pre-Intervention Interview). With hard work and commitment, Nikkia was able to accomplish her goal and shared her triumph with me during our exit interview: "I am proud of myself because I was able to get that honor roll in third and fourth grade." Furthermore, Nikkia entered the pilot study assessed using the Fountas and Pinnell literacy assessment at a level R which is the beginning of fourth grade and exited the study reading at a level T which is the beginning of fifth grade reading level.

Self-Identity

When Nikkia and I first sat down for our pre-intervention interview, she initially said "I don't know" to my first question of describing yourself. After a few seconds of thought, she was able to produce a response: "I'm funny, smart, kind, unique, intelligent, myself..." (Pre-Intervention Interview). Producing five positive adjectives about herself, Nikkia came into the intervention program with a sense of self-identity. She also went on in the interview to share, "I like myself because if someone says something about me that's not true and I know it's true then I don't care" (Pre-Intervention Interview). This is also confirmation that Nikkia's identity was established prior to her intervention experience. Throughout the entire intervention process, Nikkia demonstrated her understanding of her identity in her student work. Midway through the intervention program in Unit 6, Session 13, Nikkia wrote the following poem titled *I am Poem:*

I am beautiful, black, and bold.

I am a queen.

I am honest.

I am a leader.

I am graceful, smart, and strong.

I am me.

I am proud and funny.

I have passion and respect for others.

I am true and I am a future Queen.

I am happy to have friends and family by my side.

I am bright and I am so bright I light up the night. I am the person that stands out from the crowd because of who I am and what I do. I am proud to be black and of myself true graceful. I am proud to be brown.

Nikkia's poem evokes positive self-worth and self-image and she exited the intervention program with an unyielding sense of identity. The following are excerpts from our exit interview:

"I describe myself as a kind person. A smart, beautiful, and strong person and a loyal person and the future queen...I love myself...I'm proud of myself...I like being able to push myself to do my personal goals and help people do their goals and just help people."

"...well personally like I'm 80% West African...being a Black girl means that since I do have a part of African in my blood, that one day when I

grow up, I'm gonna go to Africa and then I just want to become a queen and I want to have a nice family…"

"Your looks doesn't define who you are. Your actions will always define who you are.…I want to be someone who can keep people on the right path and make sure that they do what they need to do in life and they don't have a hard time growing up like a hard time doing things that they wish they could do and don't end up in a bad place."

"I'm proud to be Black. I'm proud that I am strong…nowadays you have Black women that are like able to stand up like for themselves towards men…girls at the school and like the girls are strong enough to be like just because you're a boy don't mean that you just get to sit here and pick on me."

Self-Confidence

Self-Confidence is another theme that is closely related to identity with a positive emphasis on self. Nikkia came to the program equipped with identity and cultural heritage appreciation, which interrelate with self-confidence. In our initial interview, Nikkia shares, "I like myself because if someone says something about me that's not true and I know it's true then I don't care." This is a depiction of self-worth and value. She recognized that she knows the facts about herself and is not affected by outside influences. She goes on to say, "I am a leader to kids. I go over and I say like stop and I break up the fight." She understands her role within the school community and acknowledges herself as leader, mediator and problem solver.

Nikkia's self confidence only grew by the end of the program. Here she continues to reference herself as a leader in her community: "I love myself because I am a leader to a whole bunch of kids and people look up to me like they can be older than me and still believe that what I'm doing they can also do if they haven't done it yet.…just because I'm a girl don't mean that I can't do nothing" (Post-Intervention Interview). Her positive self image and worth remained steadfast.

Community

Many children value school as a shared space with friends and a place to learn. Nikkia shared a similar sentiment from her pre-intervention interview, "[school] is a place where I can learn and get smarter. And I can have friends to depend on." Here, she values school for the learning community and relationships developed. In addition to the school community, Nikkia understands the significance of community and relationship with others as she shared the following in her post-intervention interview:

"I still will go and treat [people] with respect because everybody deserves to be treated with respect. I like going to school a lot. And the reason why I like going to school is because I get it. I actually feel happy at school because you get to meet new people. You get to learn new things…"

Impacts of Decolonization Curriculum

Nikkia came to the intervention program rich in Black cultural heritage knowledge. She also came equipped with information to share with the other young ladies of the group. Along with her enthusiasm, she contributed creativity, curiosity, and joy to the space. With the wealth of assets Nikkia brought to our *Queens Gettin' Lit!* community, the intervention program cultivated a "wonderful experience" for Nikkia (Post-Intervention Interview). Nikkia affirmed the *Queens Gettin' Lit!* experience and acknowledged that learning about the historical African queens was the highlight. This affirmation is also in alignment with research literature on programs that provide culturally relevant content for students (Lane, 2018).

Chapter Six

Life is a Daily Battlefield for Black Queens

"I think if you're serious then you try to make a change. If you don't like a situation, you try to change it. Do whatever you can to change it. And if everything you do falls flat, and you can't change it, then change the way you think about it. Move to another position to look at it. In doing so, you may find a new way to change it." ~Maya Angelou

Introduction: Preparing for Battle

It is necessary to prepare young Black girls for America and the American education system. The highly researched opportunity gap demonstrates the necessity for American education to shift the content in elementary education and include accurate historical depictions of Black American history for Black girls to know that their culture is rooted in the content of Africa. As presented in previous chapters of this dissertation, curricular content does not prepare Black schoolgirls with adequate self-knowledge. Knowledge of self is important to insert into the academic institution's standards, because from a place of knowledge comes appreciation.

Not only do Black girls have to defend their minds when it comes to the information being taught and learned in American public schools, Black schoolgirls have to physically defend themselves in these learning spaces as well. Black girls are mistreated in schools on a regular basis across this country. Monique Morris's (2015) work *Pushout: The Criminalization of Black Girls in* Schools documents multiple cases of Black female students from Kindergarten to high school being physically and emotionally traumatized and ostracized by school authority figures. The most recent battlefield experience for a Black girl in school comes from the Washington Post's October 23, 2019 online article sharing a video released of a New Mexico police officer utilizing excessive force to remove an eleven-year-old student out of a middle school cafeteria (Thebault 2019). The article uses reinforcing normative behaviors of Black girls with the following statement: "…Christensen tackled the student after he and administrators said they tried for several days to get her to behave at school" (Thebault 2019). A police officer assaulted an eleven-year-old Black girl because in the eyes of white administrators a Black girl would not "behave" (Thebault 2019). Thereby making it justifiable to assault a child. The young girl is quoted in the video to admittedly be in pain stating, "I'm not resisting…Get off of me — you're hurting me" (Thebault 2019).

There is a literal battlefield Black girls must be prepared for –not the metaphorical battlefield. When the American education system consistently allows Black girls to be hurt in a space where they are to be protected and kept safe, then the education system needs changing. The change is now. A massive change of the curriculum content in the public schools is not going to happen independently. In order to see the massive shift in integrating culturally inclusive curriculum content in American public schools, school districts, administrators, and teachers must be held responsible for implementing culturally relevant content to Black female student populations. There is a need for education codes to defend and protect the Black American girls' education experience. Black girls must be able to attend school and learn information in a space that also embodies their humanity. American public schools must be held accountable.

Queens In Training

The research question that guided my work throughout this experience was: *What is the impact on urban third through fifth grade Black girls of an after school intervention program on their a) cultural heritage knowledge, b) cultural heritage agency, and c) academic progress?* The findings I present derive from the three narrative case studies presented in Chapter 4: Black Queens in the Making from Diamond Hearns, Kiara Jackson, Nikkia Edwards out of a total of fifteen study participants. Each of the focal areas within the question guided the curriculum content I created along with the questions I asked of the participants.

The following are my findings from the research based on the research question focal areas:

Cultural Heritage Knowledge

All three narrative case study participants came to the program with a sense of cultural heritage knowledge. Cultural heritage knowledge is defined as having found value and understanding of one's own geographical origin, which includes traditions and customs. Simply put, cultural heritage knowledge means knowledge of American Black history and African history prior to enslavement. Diamond, Kiara, and Nikkia knew of prominent Black people in American history; however, none of the students knew information about African queens prior to enslavement. Kiara validates this statement when she mentioned in a session video blog that she disliked being uninformed of her African royalty history. Kiara gained knowledge from *Queens Gettin' Lit!* and was able to develop a sense of identity through this historical information. During the intervention, she goes on to describe herself as a queen which is an embodiment of the knowledge she's obtained through the pilot study. Kiara's self-defined queen title also depicts her identity growing in self worth and value.

Lastly, Kiara's exit interview showed that she exited the program with historical information on Black history that she did not come to the intervention with when she was able to state facts about Black history.

Queens Gettin' Lit! Is specifically a decolonization curriculum which also sparked a desire for Nikkia to learn more information about her African heritage. She also stated in her post interview that she now wants to learn more about Black history in America and the reason behind the mistreatment of Black people. Essentially, *Queens Gettin' Lit!* supported these participants' knowledge of Black history by providing an accurate historical depiction of life prior to enslavement that many Black students are not exposed to in their public education experience. Furthermore, participants learned about Black women leaders who have helped shape America's current race relations. The collected data shows that the case study participants learned new content from the pilot study, and some were ready to learn more Black history information, while others were ready to share the information they learned with others.

Cultural Heritage Agency

Cultural heritage agency is defined by the ability and desire to share information on one's own geographical origin which includes traditions, customs, and historical facts. The majority of the case study participants shared a desire to educate others on Black history in their exit interviews. Diamond exited this study informing me of her desire to share Black history information with others during our post-intervention interview. She also shared a desire to be a leader and teach students about Black historical facts. *Queens Gettin' Lit!* activities promote leadership skill development by providing a space for participants in the group to share ideas, engage in critical thinking, and remain authentic.

Nikkia also described feeling open and free to discuss Black history with people after being in *Queens Gettin' Lit!* in her exit interview. Nikkia depicted agency when she told me during her post-intervention interview that all Black girls should be treated equally and that she wants to edcuate her peers on Black history beause she recognized that her non-Black peers do not know Black history and as a result replicated white supremacist ideology towards Black people. While *Queens Gettin' Lit!* provided a space for the case study participants to gain a sense of agency to share their Black culture with others, the concept of self-identity and self-confidence developed as themes for some of the case study participants .

Academic Progress

Academic progress is defined as the demonstration of scholastic growth and/or development. Academic progress was a peripheral outcome from the intervention. Academic progress was not the primary focus of instruction. As the goal for *Queens Gettin' Lit!* was for participants to experience the pilot study as a non-academic space otherwise known as not school. Therefore, the premise of the activities were literacy based to improve literacy skills while the actual objective of each session was to focus on Black culture and did not include measured academic performance outcomes. The participants in the study experienced academic confidence, which promotes academic progress. Primarily because students' belief in themselves increased thereby making them more likely to succeed.

The research data shows that *Queens Gettin' Lit!* supported academic confidence more than actual academic progress. For example, case study participants did demonstrate academic progress because two of three participants were honored at the school district's honor roll assembly. Additionally, all students were assessed using the Fountas and Pinnell literacy assessment and demonstrated progress. The data shows that the case study students had favorable attitudes toward academics along with academic confidence. Ultimately, Diamond, Kiara, and Nikkia shared that they value education via their interviews and session discussions but academic progress was not a clearly defined impact from the intervention study.

Fun Equates to Engagement

Findings from my study and self-reflections depict that the majority of the students' retelling of Black history and culture in schools come from their celebration and party experiences without any historical content knowledge. Many times, the primary content knowledge the participants shared was about enslavement. As a result, when participants were exposed to the enslavement unit within the decolonization curriculum content, I observed many participants reject the content and activities. Based on this data, enslavement is no longer a part of the *Queens Gettin' Lit!* curriculum.

My research data shows that effective curriculum supports the development of Black schoolgirls and moves beyond simplistic notions of appreciation such as the pizza party Kiara referenced and having posters in February . In order for Black girls to successfully experience public education, curriculum content must focus on the power and brilliance of Black women who have made a way for the subsequent generations that follow. Naturally students want to experience school in an enjoyable way, which they define as fun. While many people may hear the word fun from a student and think that the child wants to be entertained, students in fact are requesting engagement. Many participants shared with me that they wanted to have fun. It became my responsibility to develop content that informed participants of interesting content while navigating making activities that would hold their attention. This ability to balance content and engagement is a critical factor to the curriculum's model and is also the foundation for participants to be able to critically examine their own ideas. More importantly future educational researchers will need to understand this balance between rigorous content and fun identity building and strengthening content in order to continue to build from this study.

Queens Falling Into Formation

The United States of America was built upon African slaves and false narratives depicted in public elementary education curriculum and in schools throughout the country. Historically, Black people were recognized in the US Constitution as 3/5 of a human; therefore, in this country's founding documents, Black girls are not considered whole. White supremacy continues to perpetuate the false narrative of Black inferiority through the mis-education of Black minds. In 2019, governing officials in this country have yet to put in the Constitution that a Black person is 5/5 of a person and this nation should be held accountable for changing the narrative, thereby putting forth an amendment to have the documentation in writing. Carter G. Woodson (1933) captures the mis-education of the Black mind in the text *The Mis-Education of the Negro*. Woodson presents the case that Black people have developed a limited way of thinking due to the false narratives taught and embraced by American institutions and society.

The American education system has yet to break the opportunity gap that has been discussed in the literature for decades because, historically, the education system was not meant to include or educate Black minds. Just as the US Constitution only recognized 3/5 of a Black person, I propose that the American education system is teaching 3/5 of a Black child's mind based on elementary education instructional content standards. My research presents the *Queens Gettin' Lit!* decolonization curriculum as a strategy to support educating the 40% gap through targeted instruction that supports the liberation of the mind through self-knowledge. The girls presented in the narrative case studies provide evidence that Queens Gettin' Lit!'s curriculum and program is a useful resource. Diamond, Nikkia, and Kiara along with the additional twelve students were exposed to content that taught them about African queens, they read literature written to address Black girl's beauty and self-worth as well as problem solve and develop critical thinking skills through reflection via video blogs and discussions. The girls in the program accessed *Queens Gettin' Lit!* as a vehicle to attain Black history and cultural knowledge which in essence promotes mental freedom from the damage of white supremacist systems. Black history or culture is not included in curriculum textbooks across subjects from History/Social Studies to English Literature, Mathematics and Science texts; nonetheless, Black students are forced to learn European history. Hence, *Queens Gettin' Lit!* combats the current curricular structure as a decolonization curriculum and strategy to break the mis-education cycle.

The research presented depicts a curriculum purposed to inform Black third through fifth grade female students on Black history, culture, community, and self. Students had an opportunity to culturally connect with the content in the program and acknowledged the reality that they knew some Black history –primarily the recycled Black history schools across America now highlight such as Dr. Martin Luther King, Jr. and Rosa Parks, and recently even Harriet Tubman. Many of the girls had no knowledge of the origins of their Black history but were receptive and willing to learn. The participants' limited cultural knowledge was broadened by their experiences with the curriculum and in the program which transformed their self descriptions into positive depictions of self reflected in their poetry and affirmation posters from Unit 7: Love Thy Self.

Liberation! Liberation! Liberation!

Black girls must be given the opportunity to experience a safe, learning environment that provides them with information on self. Providing Black schoolgirls with the opportunity to learn about self will allow them to continue to develop critical thinking skills. Furthermore, liberation must be a part of preparing Black Queens for battle. In preparing for battle, there is a line of defense and there is a line of offense. Defense comes first, because there is a need to defend oneself on the battlefield and as the saying goes, "Defense wins games." Queens Gettin' Lit!'s instructional content prepares Black girls' minds for life's battlefield by exposing them to accurate historical content on Black women pre- and post- enslavement which is building Black girls' line of defense with self-knowledge. Next, the intervention program's decolonization curriculum also equips Black schoolgirls' minds with positive information on the Black community and culture which is preparing them offensively through self-love. In an interview with Oprah Winfrey, Lupita Nyong'o states, "Beauty only exists when we perceive it." *Queens Gettin' Lit!* curriculum content helps girls to perceive their own beauty by reading literature and examples of Black women and girls. The goal of the decolonization curriculum is also to heal the hurt and damage white supremacy has done to the mind, body, and soul of a Black woman.

The American education system was founded upon white supremacist ideals that focused on teaching patriotism and assimilation as opposed to teaching Black children to love themselves. These ideals still permeate the education system in 2019. I sat in a professional development workshop with a room full of administrators and some of them were resistant to even having a conversation about race. These administrators who were uncomfortable with discussing race among their colleagues spoke on the fact that it is even more of a challenge guiding teachers to include culturally relevant content in their lesson plans to ensure racial equity. While American public education leaders are positioned to fight equity in schools, many leaders are not comfortable to engage in dialogue on race.

Meanwhile Black girls still need to learn about themselves and then be in love with who they are to critically engage in American society. Self-love is non-existent for many Black girls in American public schools. Hence, there is so much need for authentic love of self and not superficial self-love. Decolonization interrupts American education's assimilation narrative and uproots white supremacy. My research findings demonstrate *Queens Gettin' Lit!* decolonization curriculum as an intervention that works to strategically interrupt the current American education system in order to teach Black girls to know who they are because they have come from queens who have fought with one eye and who were warriors on battlegrounds. Ase to the ancestors!

Onward March

This study is positioned to contribute to the existing literature by bringing young Black girls' voices to education research, as the majority of prior research studies focused on high school and middle school students. This study also contributes to existing literature because the intervention was implemented at an elementary school outside of school hours. Implementing the study during after school hours as opposed to during the school day may result in different engagement outcomes since the participants had long school days. Engagement results can also vary because the curriculum content may not appear to be as academically rich to students in comparison to their school day assignments and activities.

This research project also provides a snapshot of elementary aged urban Black girls' academic experiences. Education research does not have much literature from students at the critical transitional age between childhood and adolescence. Therefore, I do not know whether the participants in my study are cognizant of receiving culturally relevant instruction. Nonetheless, this provides personal accounts from elementary aged participants that will better assist researchers and education practitioners in supporting the needs of young Black girl students.

Racial identity largely determines the relationship with academic achievement because of the connection between cultural understanding and academic performance (Cokley et al., 2011). Black schoolgirls are academically disengaged due in part to a lack of culturally relevant instructional content (Pringle et. al, 2012). Educational leaders are the gatekeepers to information in the classroom and academic promotion. Black girls need strategies that support their academic experience in order to keep them in the classroom; thereby, providing them with access to education that will in turn increase academic achievement. San Francisco Unified School District has a well-documented history of Black students as the lowest performing cultural group via the California assessment data (Matthews, 2017). Black students are a priority as a result of the significant gap between standardized test outcomes and Superintendent Vincent Matthew's vision to improve Black students' academic achievement in SFUSD.

Educational researchers have begun to acknowledge the need for Black girls to have interventions to support their learning experiences just like their male counterparts (Lane, 2017). The practice of including culturally relevant instructional content based on the students in the classroom allows teachers to link academic content to what is already familiar to students as well as gives teachers the ability to face addressing oppression in the curriculum (Boutte et. al, 2010). It is essential for SFUSD schools and schools across America to incorporate the use of culturally inclusive instructional pedagogy to address the differential treatment of African American students (Paris & Alim, 2014).

The use of culturally relevant inclusion in an urban public elementary school is considered an instructional support strategy because Black girls' academic experiences are at risk. The findings from my research inform school leaders and teachers on how they might modify their instructional content design to become intentional and inclusive of affirming positive Black culture. This strategic focus on implementing equitable and culturally inclusive instruction promotes increased professional development for school site leaders and teachers on equity and a universal vision for training all instructional staff members on advancing African American achievement.

Culture plays an important role in Black students' academic behavior and public school districts should take notice and develop culturally inclusive pedagogy that honors "Africentric values" (Shin, 2011). Furthermore, all students would benefit from curricular content that pushed them to think critically of the oppressive narratives and white supremacy based norms that American culture and society have accepted. Most importantly, in order to keep Black students engaged in schools, they must be able to see themselves positively reflected in their academic experience.

The work of supporting instructors to include Black cultural references into curriculum content is transforming classroom teachers into becoming social justice change agents. bell hooks (1994), a feminist theorist, presents examples of transformational leadership in *Teaching to Transgress: Education as the Practice of Freedom* using two main pedagogies: Engaged Pedagogy and Transformative Pedagogy. hooks is an education practitioner who advises educators to apply both pedagogies in their teaching practice and changing how they interact with students (hooks, 1994). Implementing culturally equitable instructional content is pushing teachers to shift their vision of practice to a cultural approach to learning. Cultural inclusion is also grounded in transforming the teaching practice. For many educators, the act of modifying the curriculum content in order to be more inclusive of all students represented in the classroom and creating community in order to engage students of color on a personal level in order to have a rich dialogue to learn from on another is daunting.

Teachers must become intentional about including Black culture into lesson content which shifts classroom instructors' mentality toward the way they interact with their students. Culturally inclusive content supports hooks acknowledgment of the importance of developing relationships with students (hooks, 1994). Implementing this type of engaged pedagogy also takes a level of understanding self that is necessary for teachers to embrace when educating as a practice of liberation. hooks states, "[Educators] who embrace the challenge of self-actualization will be better able to create pedagogical practices that engages students, providing them with ways of knowing that enhance their capacity" (hooks, 1994, p.22).

In addition to Engaged Pedagogy, hooks discusses Transformative Pedagogy which takes a level of consciousness on the part of the instructor to implement. For many educators as well as students of the institution who decide to implement this pedagogy, the experience is an uncomfortable shift of power from being the authoritative instructor and passive learner to both parties sharing content and knowledge with one another. It is important to acknowledge that shifting teaching practices is challenging and teachers need support through the process of self-actualization and integrating cultural inclusion into instructional content.

An Army of Black Queens

Queens Gettin' Lit! is a decolonization curriculum purposed to prepare future Black queens to navigate life's battleground. The findings presented depict students learning about Black history and culture to gain greater cultural knowledge and as a result students developed a sense of self-identity. This self-knowledge gain is a defense against the typical teaching approaches that reinforce oppressive, white supremacy based normative behavior standards and expectations that negatively impact Black schoolgirls academically and behaviorally. The findings also showed participants using positive affirming language about themselves in support of developing self-love. In fact, this is the curriculum's offensive strategy in combating life's battlefield experience within the public education system.

The San Francisco Unified School District along with countless other districts across America must begin to embrace modifying their curricular content to become intentional and inclusive of affirming positive Black culture, which cultivates the development of Black pride and self-identity in order to refute negative stereotypes and biases that enter into public school classrooms. Culturally Relevant Pedagogy allows teachers to link academic content to what is already familiar to students as well as gives teachers the ability to face addressing oppression in the curriculum (Boutte et. al, 2010). Research also proves that students are engaged with lessons that are pertinent to their experiences through Culturally Relevant Pedagogy (Sampson and Garrison-Wade, 2011). *Queens Gettin' Lit!* decolonization curriculum is a culturally relevant

91

model and reference tool for school districts, nonprofit and for-profit organizations to utilize in support of the social justice movement towards building an army of future Black queens.

REFERENCES

Annamma, S. A., Anyon, Y., Joseph, N. M., Farrar, J., Greer, E., Downing, B., & Simmons, J. (2016). Black girls and school discipline: The complexities of being overrepresented and understudied. *Urban Education,* 0042085916646610.

Boutte, Gloria, Kelly-Jackson, Charlease, & Johnson, George Lee. (2010). Culturally relevant teaching in science classrooms: Addressing academic achievement, cultural competence, and critical consciousness. International Journal of Multicultural Education, 12(2).

Brown, T. M. (2007). Lost and Turned Out: Academic, Social, and Emotional Experiences of Students Excluded From School. *Urban Education,* 42(5), 432–455. https://doi.org/10.1177/0042085907304947

Chavous, T. M., Bernat, D. H., Schmeelk-Cone, K., Caldwell, C. H., Kohn-Wood, L., & Zimmerman, M. A. (2003). Racial Identity and Academic Attainment Among African American Adolescents. *Child Development,* 74(4), 1076–1090. https://doi.org/10.1111/1467-8624.00593

Cokley, K., McClain, S., Jones, M., & Johnson, S. (2011). A Preliminary Investigation of Academic Disidentification, Racial Identity, and Academic Achievement Among African American Adolescents. *The High School Journal; Chapel Hill,* 95(2), 54–68.

Collins, P. H. (1990). *Black feminist thought: Knowledge, consciousness, and the politics of empowerment.* New York: Routledge.

Evans-Winters, V. (2005). Teaching black girls: Resiliency in urban classrooms. New York:

Peter Lang.

Evans-Winters, V. (2007). 11. Urban African American Female Students and Educational Resiliency. *Counterpoints, 306,* 167–178.

Evans-Winters, V. E., & Esposito, J. (2010). Other people's daughters: critical race feminism and black girls' education. Educational Foundations, 14.

Howard, A., Patterson, A., Kinloch, V., Burkhard, T., & Randall, R. (2016). The *Black Women's Gathering Place* : Reconceptualising a curriculum of place/space. *Gender and Education,* 28(6), 756–768. https://doi.org/10.1080/09540253.2016.1221895

Howard, T. C., & Navarro, O. (2016). Critical Race Theory 20 Years Later: Where Do We Go From Here? *Urban Education,* 51(3), 253–273.
https://doi.org/10.1177/0042085915622541

Jacobs, C. E. ., chjacobs@gse.upenn.ed. (2016). Developing the "Oppositional Gaze": Using Critical Media Pedagogy and Black Feminist Thought to Promote Black Girls' Identity Development. *Journal of Negro Education,* 85(3), 225–238.

Khalifa, M. (2010). Validating Social and Cultural Capital of Hyperghettoized At-Risk Students. *Education and Urban Society,* 42(5), 620–646.
https://doi.org/10.1177/0013124510366225

Khalifa, M. A., Gooden, M. A., & Davis, J. E. (2016). Culturally responsive school leadership: A synthesis of the literature. *Review of Educational Research,* 86(4), 1272–1311.

Ladson-Billings, G. (1995). Toward a Theory of Culturally Relevant Pedagogy. *American Educational Research Journal,32(3),* 465-491. Retrieved from http://www.jstor.org/stable/1163320

Lane, M. (2017). Reclaiming Our Queendom: Black Feminist Pedagogy and the Identity Formation of African American Girls. Equity & Excellence in Education, 50(1), 13–24. h ttps://doi.org/10.1080/10665684.2016.1259025

Lane, M. (2018). "For Real Love": How Black Girls Benefit from a Politicized Ethic of Care. *International Journal of Educational Reform,* 27(3), 269–290. https://doi.org/10.1177/105678791802700303

Langhout, R., & Mitchell, C. (2008). Engaging contexts: Drawing the link between student and teacher experiences of the hidden curriculum. *Journal of Community & Applied Social Psychology,* 18(6), 593-614.

Lindsay-Dennis, L. (2015). Black Feminist-Womanist Research Paradigm: Toward a Culturally Relevant Research Model Focused on African American Girls. *Journal of Black Studies,* 46(5), 506–520. https://doi.org/10.1177/0021934715583664

Matthews, V. (2017). *The First Ninety Days - Listening and Learning Report.* [online] San Francisco: San Francisco Unified School District, pp.1-35. Available at: https://www.boarddocs.com/ca/sfusd/Board.nsf/files/AT54FG0B5476/$file/SFUSD%2090%20Day%20report%2017-1114%20v1.docx%20(3).pdf [Accessed 22 Mar. 2018].

Mendez, L. M. R., & Knoff, H. M. (2003). Who Gets Suspended from School and Why: A Demographic Analysis of Schools and Disciplinary Infractions in a Large School District. *Education and Treatment of Children,* 26(1), 30–51.

Morris, E. W. (2007). "Ladies" or "Loudies"?: Perceptions and Experiences of Black Girls in Classrooms. Youth & Society, 38(4), 490–515. https://doi.org/10.1177/0044118X06296778

Morris, M. W. (2016). *Pushout: The Criminalization of Black Girls in Schools.* New York: The New Press.

NAEP Reading: National Achievement-Level Results. (n.d.). Retrieved May 19, 2018, from https://www.nationsreportcard.gov/reading_2017/#/nation/achievement?grade=4

Nyachae, T. M. (2016). Complicated contradictions amid Black feminism and millennial Black women teachers creating curriculum for Black girls. *Gender and Education,* 28(6), 786–806. https://doi.org/10.1080/09540253.2016.1221896

Paris, D., & Alim, H. S. (2014). What are we seeking to sustain through culturally sustaining pedagogy? A loving critique forward. *Harvard Educational Review, 84*(1), 85–100. https://doi.org/10.17763/haer.84.1.982l873k2ht16m77

Price-Dennis, D. (2016). Developing curriculum to support black girls' literacies in digital spaces. English Education, 48(4), 337-361.

Pringle, R., Brkich, K., Adams, T., West-Olatunii, C., & Archer-Banks, D. (2012). Factors influencing elementary teachers' positioning of african american girls as science and mathematics learners. School Science and Mathematics, 112(4), 217-229.

Sampson, D., & Garrison-Wade, D. F. (2011). Cultural vibrancy: Exploring the preferences of African American children toward culturally relevant and non-culturally relevant lessons. The Urban Review, 43(2), 279–309. https://doi.org/10.1007/s11256-010-0170-x

Shin, R. Q. (2011). The influence of Africentric values and neighborhood satisfaction on the academic self-efficacy of African American elementary school children. *Journal of Multicultural Counseling and Development,* 39(4), 218–228. https://doi.org/10.1002/j.2161-1912.2011.tb00636.x

Solórzano, D. G., & Yosso, T. J. (2002). Critical race methodology: Counter-storytelling as an analytical framework for education research. *Qualitative Inquiry,* 8(1), 23–44.

Taylor, K.Y. (2017). How we get free: Black feminism and the combahee river collective. Chicago: Haymarket Books.

Thebault, R. (2019, October 23). Video shows police officer tackling an 11-year-old girl he accused of being 'disruptive' at school. *Washington Post.* Retrieved from https://www.washingtonpost.com/education/2019/10/23/video-shows-police-officer-tackling-an-year-old-girl-he-accused-being-disruptive-school/

Wiggan, G., & Watson, M. J. (2016). Teaching the Whole Child: The Importance of Culturally Responsiveness, Community Engagement, and Character Development in High Achieving African American Students. *The Urban Review,* 48(5), 766–798. https://doi.org/10.1007/s11256-016-0377-6

Wun, C. (2016). Unaccounted foundations: Black girls, anti-Black racism, and punishment in schools. *Critical Sociology,* 42(4–5), 737–750.

Zirkel, S., & Johnson, T. (2016). Mirror, Mirror on the Wall: A Critical Examination of the Conceptualization of the Study of Black Racial Identity in Education. *Educational Researcher,* 45(5), 301–311. https://doi.org/10.3102/0013189X16656938

www.ingramcontent.com/pod-product-compliance
Lightning Source LLC
Chambersburg PA
CBHW051539120626

46551CB00013B/1297